In Praise of
DESSERT LOVERS' CHOICE

"The recipes in this book will definitely fill a need that is constantly expressed by those who have diabetes. Most people with diabetes are looking for ways to incorporate their favorite desserts into the diabetes meal plan. These diabetes-friendly recipes represent a wide variety of family favorites that will appeal to a person with diabetes of any age who is craving a special dessert for a special occasion."

—Connie Crawley, M.S., R.D., L.D., public service associate, University of Georgia

"This recipe collection is no ordinary cookbook. It's a heartfelt story of the interrelationship between food, family, and life. The journey that led Yvonne Sanders-Butler to develop and share these wonderful alternative recipes will enable everyone to again enjoy the comfort foods that recall our youth, a sense of belonging, and the memories that we cling to. Each recipe has been carefully analyzed to provide calorie and macronutrient content. State-of-the-art carbohydrate counts are also included, enabling those challenged with diabetes to make informed choices. Recipes using soy-based proteins will enhance the dietary intake of phytochemicals known to have preventative, as well as treatment effects on many disease conditions. These heart-healthy recipes will once again bring people and families together and promote a healthy lifestyle for our loved ones and ourselves."

—Kay Umeakunne, M.S., R.D., L.D.

D0731568

DESSERT LOVERS' CHOICE

NATURALLY SWEET, NATURALLY DELICIOUS

Yvonne Sanders-Butler, Ed.D.

HP Books

An HP Book
Published by the Penguin Group
Penguin Group (USA) Inc.
375 Hudson Street, New York, New York 10014, USA
Penguin Group (Canada), 10 Alcorn Avenue, Toronto, Ontario M4V 3B2, Canada
(a division of Pearson Penguin Canada Inc.)
Penguin Books Ltd., 80 Strand, London WC2R 0RL, England
Penguin Group Ireland, 25 St. Stephen's Green, Dublin 2, Ireland
(a division of Penguin Books Ltd.)
Penguin Group (Australia), 250 Camberwell Road, Camberwell, Victoria 3124, Australia
(a division of Pearson Australia Group Pty. Ltd.)
Penguin Books India Pvt. Ltd., 11 Community Centre, Panchsheel Park,
New Delhi—110 017, India
Penguin Group (NZ), cnr. Airborne and Rosedale Roads, Albany, Auckland 1310,
New Zealand (a division of Pearson New Zealand Ltd.)
Penguin Books (South Africa) (Pty.) Ltd., 24 Sturdee Avenue, Rosebank,
Johannesburg 2196, South Africa
Penguin Books Ltd., Registered Offices: 80 Strand, London WC2R 0RL, England

PRINTING HISTORY
HP trade paperback edition/May 2005

HP is a registered trademark of Penguin Group (USA) Inc.

Library of Congress Cataloging-in-Publication Data

Sanders-Butler, Yvonne.
    Dessert lovers' choice / Yvonne Sanders-Butler.
        p. cm.
    Includes bibliographical references and index.
    ISBN 1-55788-466-8
    1. Desserts.   I. Title.

    TX773.S3138 2005
    641.8'6—dc22

                                                    2004062554

PRINTED IN THE UNITED STATES OF AMERICA

10   9   8   7   6   5   4   3   2   1

To my loving mother, Ruth Mae Sanders, for holding my hand and having the patience to teach me how to make cookie dough at the age of four. Years later, you held my hand once again while I modified our family dessert recipes to make them healthier, which became the basis for this book. The incredible bond we already shared was strengthened further by this experience, and I will cherish it forever. I am the person I am today largely because of all you have given me. It is a debt I can never truly repay, only acknowledge by dedicating this book to you. I love you, Mom, and I will always miss you.

ACKNOWLEDGMENTS

Thank You:

To God be the glory! Because of You, I am; and because of You, I will always be blessed.

To my Daddy Bo, West Sanders. You will always be my hero. Daddy, you have always made us girls feel that we could have it all. I believed you! Your love and support will always sustain me and I will always love you, Daddy.

To my dearest husband, Floyd. I love you for supporting me in all of my endeavors for the past twenty-five years.

To my loving son, Denard, my cowboy. Life has great things in store for you. Always place God first and everything else you want or need will follow.

To my six beautiful sisters: Dorothy (Dot), Lillie (Jim), Shirley (Shelley), Doris (Mick), Betty, and Annette (Wanky), you have always supported me in all of my endeavors without reservation. You girls are the greatest and I love you.

To all of my brothers-in-law, especially Fulton (for having my back when I needed you), Thaddeus (the man with the master plan) Roosevelt, Mack, and Kenny for their unconditional love and support.

To Johnnie, I will always remember you being there for me in the early years when I needed you the most.

Luke, God has given my parents a son and us a brother. You are a testament of God's love and grace.

To my sisters-in-law, especially Hazel, Sadie (my girl), Charlie Mae, and Zerlene for all of your support and encouragement.

To my nieces and nephews, especially my "Lil" Star and Brady Boy, remember that age is nothing but a number. Live your life to the fullest and never quit dreaming.

What would life be without your best girlfriend? I love you, Rose "Danny" Johnson. Thank you, Danny, for being a wonderful friend and a sister.

To the girls whom I could not love more if I had given birth to them: Anjulia, Simone, Nina, and Tanjala. The world has great things in store for you. You are the greatest.

I would be remiss if I did not give a special thanks to these very unique ladies whom I call the "Naturally Yours Faith-Based Team." I could not have done it without you. A very special thank you goes out to Hazel Lucas, Tanyetta Goodjiones, Alfreda Trawick, and Sadie Butler for always making the connection and the deadlines.

Special kudos to Ms. Joanne Cooper, Ife Green, Judy Khan, Mary Young, and Frenchella Thibedeaux. No project is successful without the love and support of great friends and colleagues.

Jemel and Marie, I would like to thank you for all of your love, support, and encouragement through this process.

Thank you, Mae, for your love and prayers throughout this entire process. Thanks to my adopted brothers, Lonzo and Lonnie, for not letting me stop even when I did not think I had the energy to go on. To the Browns Mill faculty, staff, parents, and students, I appreciate you for all of your support and love. You are the true meaning of family. I also would like to thank you for testing all of my recipes.

Thanks to two of my very special friends, Lamar and Audrey Williams, for donating their lovely countryside home for two days to shoot the layout for the recipes.

Thanks to Earl Thomas and his beautiful wife, Pamela, of RMT Construction, Inc., for opening their beautiful home for yet another photo shoot.

And a thanks to Herman and Vernessa Cunningham for not only allowing me to shoot more photos in your home, but also for supporting Floyd and me with your love and prayers throughout this entire process. You both have a very special place in my heart.

Thank you, Mike Hall, for consulting with me on my vegetarian dessert recipes. You are the greatest.

To the Naturally Yours & More Support staff:

Thaddeus Mayfield, I am blessed to not only have you in my family but also as my business consultant. You have encouraged me to grow even when it was painful and helped me to go beyond those ordinary boundaries to succeed.

Lorine, I can never thank you for the zillions of hours you have spent researching and analyzing recipes. Your love and compassion for mankind has certainly inspired me to continue my race.

Nekita Johnson, you are worth your weight in gold. Thank you for keeping me organized and focused.

Kay Umeakunne, your nutritional expertise has been invaluable to me. I thank you for your spirit and your support.

Curtis Bunn, you are always at the top of your game and I admire you. As an author and veteran writer, your advice and many hours of feedback have been priceless to me. I know I can never repay you, but I thank you from the bottom of my heart.

To Hazel Lucas, you have been with me through this entire process and no one knows better than you how many times we have reworked and rethought this process. Thank you for being my sounding board and for providing me with professional and educational support and feedback 24/7.

Cheryl Thomas, you are truly a gifted artist in every sense. What would a girl do without the best makeup artist in the business? Thank you for signing on with Naturally Yours in our humble stage of inception.

To Terence Li, my photographer and a true professional: You have done an extraordinary job of capturing these desserts on film. The pictures say it all.

To Jay Lee, my stylist. You are so creative and supportive. Your taste is impeccable, whether it is being creative with food or fashion.

To Sharon Ritchey and her assistant, Kristen Ball, for assisting me to tell my story. I would like to take this opportunity to thank you for a job well done.

To Carol Helms, project director of the Metro Atlanta American Diabetes Association. Thanks for reaching out to me and sharing Connie Crawley with me. Thank you for the difference you are making in lives each day.

To Connie Crawley, thank you for sharing and caring when I needed it most. You gave me information and material that was very helpful in my quest to become more knowledgeable about diabetes.

TABLE OF CONTENTS

FOREWORD

Although I grew up in the New York City area, my father's hometown, Orangeburg, South Carolina, has profoundly shaped my childhood. Many of my grandmother's talents come from her Southern roots, just one of which was the art of cooking and baking. Some of my fondest childhood memories are of feasting at family gatherings and celebrations. I remember my sisters, cousins, and I suppressing our laughter during my grandfather's long blessing before we could dig into those mouth-watering, flavorful dishes and pastries on the table before us.

During one Christmas break from college, I tried to shadow my grandmother in her kitchen in an attempt to document her recipes, but the teacups, pinches, and teaspoons she used for measuring ingredients were not listed in my college textbooks. I have often regretted not capturing my grandmother's wonderful recipes for coconut cake, custard pie, and pound cake. Fortunately, Yvonne Butler's compilation of recipes provides me with a second chance to capture some of those forgotten delicacies from my childhood, including coconut cake and custard pie! In addition, the "Mom's Choice" chapter includes snacks that children will enjoy preparing as well as eating.

The healthful desserts presented here are sorely needed. With the United States' increasing rates of heart disease, diabetes, cancer, hypertension, and our national obesity epidemic, we are not preparing our children for a healthy future. Rather, we turn to doctors and diet pills to do what we choose not to. Let's face it: Most of us need to make a complete lifestyle change by modifying our eating behavior and increasing our physical activity. Unfortunately, many diets eliminate desserts and pastries altogether. As a dietician, I can tell you that this need not be the case. With careful planning and the approval of your dietitian and physician, you can occasionally include healthfully prepared desserts in your meal plan, and Yvonne's book provides many delectable choices.

For your convenience, *Dessert Lovers' Choice* includes a nutrient analysis complete with servings yielded. Many of these recipes include soy products and a reduced amount of sugar, sodium, and fat. In your quest for a healthier lifestyle, remember to make meal pattern changes gradually, watch your serving sizes, increase your activity, and drink water. You can take care of yourself and indulge in an occasional treat, thanks to the wonderful recipes in *Dessert Lovers' Choice*.

—Lorine Phillips Bizzell, R.D., M.S., M.B.A.

INTRODUCTION

What's more American than apple pie, hamburgers, and French fries? How about arthritis, asthma, diabetes, and heart disease? Because of Americans' love of the foods in the first list, we've seen a rise in the diseases in the second. Sadly, these are just a few of the health complications related to overweight and obesity. According to the Centers for Disease Control (CDC), you can reduce your risk for all of the above illnesses if you maintain a healthy weight by eating nutritious foods and exercising. For most people, extreme measures such as drugs and surgery are unnecessary. Why then, did the CDC find that in 1999, 61 percent of Americans were still overweight or obese?

One of many answers is in the foods we eat. We've all seen the Food Guide Pyramid constructed of suggested servings of healthful foods such as grains, produce, meats, and dairy. However, few of us use it. In fact, according to the U.S. Department of Health and Human Services, in 2001, only 3 percent of Americans met four of the pyramid's five guidelines. In the small tip of the pyramid you find fats, oils, and sweets, but no daily servings are suggested. Rather, we are warned to use them "sparingly." Ah, the call for self-restraint and self-deprivation. Few of us have mastered the art of self-control when it comes to food. After all, life is short. Why deprive yourself? Well, life may be shorter than you anticipated if you don't. I learned this the hard way—through personal experience.

In 1996, after having dinner out with a friend, I noticed that my left eye was aching. As the evening wore on, my eye became red and painful, and later that night, I went to the emergency room. After the doctor on duty had taken my vitals, he asked me if I'd forgotten to take my hypertension medication that day. I panicked. I informed the doctor that I didn't take any medication. "You do now," he sternly replied. "Your blood pressure is 200 over 140, and you are on the verge of having a stroke."

I was stunned. I followed the doctor's orders and took the prescribed medication, but I was depressed and eating myself into a coma. Eventually, one of my sisters, a physician who received her training at the Mayo Clinic, suggested that I go to the Mayo for a major work-up. After a full week of being stuck, poked, and probed, their diagnosis was that I was fifty pounds overweight. In sum, I had paid fourteen thousand dollars simply to be told that I was fat!

Fifty pounds is a lot of weight. I was frightened by the prospect of having to lose so much body weight, and didn't know how I would give up the many desserts that I loved. Once again, my sisters were at my side. They helped me find a weight-loss support group, and I began to understand why I loved sweets so much. It was a revelation to learn that many people, like myself, are truly addicted to sugar and foods high in carbohydrates. Thus, the healing process began, and I started to gain control over my eating habits without giving up desserts.

Most people eliminate desserts from their diets when they are trying to lose weight or eat more healthfully. However, for healthy individuals trying to eat better, giving up on desserts entirely is not necessary. Of course, if you have a medical condition with dietary restrictions, you should consult your doctor before deviating from your prescribed diet.

Five years ago, when I began looking for ways to include the foods I enjoy in my diet without risking my health, I found natural ingredients to be an alternative. Altering my favorite dessert recipes to include natural ingredients allowed me to enjoy desserts in moderation and still lose the weight. In fact, the fifty pounds that once overwhelmed me are now gone, and I still enjoy peanut butter cookies, custard pie, and my mom's famous chocolate muffins. Not only did I lose weight, my health improved dramatically. I was so excited, I felt the need to share my findings with others, and the first people who came to mind were my students.

As the principal of an elementary school serving over one thousand children, I recognized my former eating habits in my students. I observed that many of the children rarely ate vegetables, and that the most popular days for buying school lunches featured hamburgers and French fries (or other equally fatty foods) on the menu. I also noticed that the children who purchased extra portions were already overweight. A closer look revealed that the same students traded food in the cafeteria with the zeal of Wall Street brokers. Cookies, fruit punch, chocolate milk, and potato chips had become currency, and it was changing hands rapidly.

One day while observing such "cafeteria deals," I decided that I had to help these children make a change. I was on lunch duty, watching a young boy trade his baseball cards for his friends' desserts and fries. As I looked at his young overweight body, I was reminded of myself as a child, bartering for extra food to quell some insatiable appetite. Because he looked so helpless relinquishing his last baseball card in exchange for a brownie, I resolved to do something right then and there for my students. With the help of my staff and the PTA, I began the process of creating a sugar-free school.

The results were remarkable. During the first year of the program, students didn't trade lunches as much, and those who started the school year with extra weight began to slim down. Office referrals, which are always at their peak after breakfast and lunch, decreased by 30 percent, and teachers reported that students were concentrating better in class. Students' test scores improved markedly, and the guidance counselor noted a 25 percent decrease in referrals for conflicts between students. I then took my findings to the parents in the form of seminars and workshops that addressed the many health risks, such as juvenile diabetes, that diets high in sugar pose to our children. My message was well received, and parents began preparing healthier lunches for their children.

I never intended to write a book. I started a healthier lifestyle to overcome my personal health challenges, such as obesity, hypertension, and arthritis. During this process, this book was born. It has been a wonderful experience for me.

I want to stress, however, that this is not a diet book. Rather, it offers a healthier approach to eating desserts and sweets by substituting standard high-fat, high-cholesterol, and high-sugar ingredients with natural, healthier ones that reduce all of these items.

After several years of extensive research, I have learned that one can eat all enjoyable foods in moderation, especially desserts, if they are properly prepared. However, such desserts are not readily available in America's mainstream culinary culture. It is my hope that by providing you with easy-to-prepare recipes for delicious desserts such as carrot cake, sugar cookies, double fudge pie, and cheesecake, you'll see how possible it is to enjoy truly sweet treats without compromising your waistline or your health.

Here's to your health!

Best wishes,
Yvonne Butler-Sanders

A WORD ON RECIPE DEVELOPMENT, NATURAL INGREDIENTS, AND NUTRITIONAL DATA

Several years ago, in an effort to control my weight and literally save my life, I gave up eating desserts. I felt deprived and left out of many social events. I avoided making treats for my family and friends, something I loved to do. I soon realized that denying myself the pleasure of cooking and enjoying sweets was not realistic over the long term. Healthy eating or living with a restricted diet should not have to be about sacrifice or deprivation. Food is important to both our mental and physical well-being. We build relationships around family meals, treasured family recipes, and the satisfaction we feel when our families are well fed. Yet how do you balance these fundamental desires with healthy eating?

The answer for my family and me was to change how I thought about eating and cooking in general. I created this collection of recipes to help manage a series of health problems, including obesity, allergy sensitivity, and diabetes—all of which afflict not just my family, but millions of Americans. However, this cookbook is not meant to be a panacea for our nation's growing food and health issues. Rather, it represents what I have learned about how to incorporate foods that I love into my diet and the diet of my family in a naturally healthy way.

Natural Ingredients

As I started making a lifestyle change to improve my health, I began to look at the foods I prepared, especially desserts, and the ingredients I used to prepare them. Changing the ingredients I used to make family desserts was a challenge for me. Many of my dessert recipes had been passed down from generation to generation. Even the slightest change of ingredients could destroy several lifetimes of tradition. How could I be true to my mother and all of my ancestors if I replaced the traditional ingredients that had always been used in our cakes and pies?

But I knew that if I were to be successful in making a healthy lifestyle change, I would have to find ways to modify the desserts. I began to extensively research how natural ingredients benefit our health and began exploring how I could incorporate them into my favorite desserts. I read much literature related to healthy cooking, subscribed to many health magazines, and frequented grocery and health-food stores that carried natural and organic ingredients for cooking and baking. Shortly thereafter, I began to experiment with some of the ingredients to make desserts.

As I began to modify my recipes, I did not immediately replace all of the ingredients. I prioritized the ingredients and their significance to each recipe. I then modified one ingredient at a time so that I would be able to determine its effect on the recipe. Each time I made the recipe, I added another natural ingredient.

As I continued to modify traditional desserts to create my own healthy desserts using natural ingredients, I began to test them on family and friends. They could not believe that the desserts had been made using natural sugars, flours, butters, and oils. They wanted to follow me home to see how I made these recipes, and oftentimes they did. I believed that I had found the key to healthy, baked desserts without sacrificing taste. Following are the organic ingredients and natural sweeteners I use in my recipes, and why I feel that they are so important to maintaining good health.

WHERE TO FIND NATURAL INGREDIENTS

If you do not find the ingredients you need at your local grocery store, consult with your store manager. Many store managers will order the products for you.

I would also suggest your local health food stores as well. I have provided a list of sources beginning on page 127 to help you locate some of these ingredients as well. Make sure you read the fine print on the labels of all ingredients to ensure you're not getting any unwelcome surprises—like hidden fats or sugars.

NATURAL SWEETENERS

According to the latest research, the average American consumes as much as two pounds of sugar a week! Many studies have illustrated the significance that excess sugar and fat plays in the development of dental cavities, obesity, and other chronic diseases occurring in record numbers in the United States. Before starting this wellness journey, I was unaware of how much sugar I consumed each day. After extensive research, I realized that sugar is in almost everything we eat, not only in the desserts that we buy or prepare. Sugar is in natural fruits, grains, and vegetables. I was astonished to learn how much sugar is in breakfast cereal, French fries, and sodas. Canned foods also contain high percentages of sugar. I have not used any white sugar or alternative sweeteners in any of the recipes in this book because I believe that the more natural and less-processed sugars are sweeter to taste; therefore, less natural sugar is used in my recipes. Alternative or non-nutritive sweeteners, such as aspartame and saccharin, add an intense sweetness with few calories to food; however, they do not function in the same way that natural sugar does in baking desserts. Unlike alternative sweeteners, natural sugar is a major contributor to the volume, texture, browning, and tenderness of each delicious product.

What Are Natural Sweeteners?
When natural sweeteners are used, it reduces the amount of sugar in most recipes by one-third, and sometimes even by half. After modifying many of my dessert recipes with natural sweeteners, I decided which natural sweeteners worked best for me. Most of my recipes require dry (granulated) sweeteners such as natural turbinado sugar, maple sugar, and organic sugar. Liquid sweeteners such as maple syrup, unsulphured molasses, and natural sugar-free fruit juice also work well in suggested recipes. I would not suggest the use of liquid sweeteners as a substitute for dry sweeteners unless specified in the recipe. Even though all sugars function

the same way, I consider the following as natural sweeteners because they do not undergo as extensive processing as white refined and brown sugars.

Maple sugar, which is twice as sweet as granulated white sugar, is the result of continuing to boil maple tree sap until the liquid has almost entirely evaporated.

Turbinado sugar is raw sugar that has been steam-cleaned and centrifuged. The coarse turbinado crystals are blond-colored and have a delicate molasses flavor.

Fruits are very healthy foods that are naturally sweetened by their own juices. I use natural and frozen fruits in many of my recipes. I only use frozen fruits that do not contain preservatives or added sugars. I do add small amounts of natural sweeteners because they are necessary to create wonderful recipes.

Various brands of sweeteners or sugars can be found in your local grocery stores. As you begin to cook with them, you will decide which ones you like best.

I, personally, do not use honey because it is sweeter than white sugar and works just like white sugar does in my body: It causes me to crave other sugars and carbohydrates.

FLOUR

When I was a child, my mother never used cake flour. She always used all-purpose white flour and self-rising white flour. Until four years ago, I, too, didn't use any other flours. (Oh, I did cheat a bit. I used cake flour for selected cakes.) I'd like to share with you what I learned about flour.

Whole wheat flour contains wheat germ, which means that it also has higher fiber, nutritional, and fat contents. Because of the latter, it should be stored in the refrigerator to prevent rancidity.

Cake or pastry flour is a fine-textured, soft-wheat flour with a high starch content. It makes particularly tender cakes and pastries.

Oat flour is made from groats that have been ground into powder. It contains no gluten, so in baked goods that need to rise, like yeast bread, oat flour must be combined with a rising flour. Today, whole oats are still used as animal fodder. Human beings don't usually consume them until after the oats have been cleaned, toasted, hulled, and cleaned again, after which time they become oat groats.

Soy flour is made from roasted soybeans ground into a fine powder. There are three kinds of soy flour available:

- Natural or full-fat, which contains the natural oils found in the soybean
- Defatted, from which the oils are removed during processing
- Lecithinated, which has added lecithin

This finely ground flour is made from soybeans and, unlike many flours, is high in protein (twice that of wheat flour) and low in carbohydrates. Soy flour is usually mixed with other flours rather than used alone. It has a wide variety of uses, from baking desserts to binding sauces. In Japan, it's very popular for making confections. Soy flour is sold in health-food stores—sometimes under the name *kinako*—and in some supermarkets. I only use soy flour in recipes that are strong in flavor like my Chocolate Cake, Black Cake, and Fruitcake. I do not recommend using soy flour in plain cakes, pies, or muffins.

Unbleached all-purpose white flour is a wheat flour that has been carefully milled into a white flour; it retains much of its original vitamins and minerals. It is not as refined as regular white flours, resulting in more fiber in the finished product.

Organic white flour is organically grown with no added chemicals.

Self-rising unbleached white flour is made from soft, red wheat with salt and aluminum-free baking powder added. Do not add additional salt, baking powder, or baking soda when using self-rising flour. I do not suggest that you combine self-rising and unbleached white flours with other flours. Only use it in recipes that call for self-rising white flour.

Whole grain flour, like whole-wheat pastry flour, is made from very soft wheat and milled into a fine flour. Do not substitute whole-wheat flour for whole-wheat pastry flour. The resulting cake will be more like dry bread.

Tips for Baking with Flour
1. Keep flour in the refrigerator in an airtight container to ensure its freshness.
2. Sift your flour, especially whole grain flour, as you add it to the ingredients, unless the recipe specifies otherwise.
3. Carefully measure your flours. Accurate measurements produce the best results.

DAIRY ALTERNATIVES

For a long time I did not know I was lactose-intolerant. No matter how bloated I became after eating ice cream or cheese, the taste was better than the misery that followed. I could not imagine life without ice cream, butter, cream cheese, or milk.

Many people incorrectly believe that if their diet does not include dairy products, their bodies will not receive the required amounts of protein, vitamin D, and calcium. The flip side of the coin is that many dairy foods tend to be high in saturated fatty acids, which doctors say increase our risk of cancer.

Guess what? There are some great dairy alternatives. Yes, I know you are saying that you have tried some of dairy alternatives such as rice milk, soy milk, soy cream, and butter, and they just do not taste as good as the dairy products. Well, those were my exact thoughts until I started to experiment with different brands and began using soy products as I modified recipes to make my desserts.

A note of caution: Many brand names are cashing in on all-natural health food titles. When purchasing your ingredients, please read your labels carefully.

Milk: Dairy-free milk substitutes can be found in most local grocery stores, and many different brands are available.

Soy Milk: Is one alternative to cow's milk. Higher in protein than cow's milk, this milky, iron-rich liquid is a nondairy product made by pressing ground, cooked soybeans. Soy milk is cholesterol-free and low in fat and sodium. It makes an excellent milk substitute for anyone with a milk allergy and can be purchased with added flavors such as chocolate and vanilla. Although it is low in calcium, many milk substitutes are often fortified with calcium. Soy milk has a tendency to curdle when mixed with acidic ingredients such as lemon juice and wine; it's intentionally curdled in the making of tofu. Soy buttermilk is also really easy to make. Just add 2 teaspoons of vinegar or lemon juice to 1 cup of soymilk.

Soy Margarine: In many of my recipes I use oil, but when only a good butter or margarine will do, I use nondairy margarines and butters made from soybeans. In many recipes, I indicate melting the margarine. I suggest you microwave it for about 30 seconds, then leave it in the microwave until ready for use to help it stay liquid.

I have read many health magazines and books about soy products, and I have learned that soy helps to prevent diseases such as breast cancer, heart disease, hypertension, arthritis, diabetes, and osteoporosis. Since I suffer from several of these diseases, I have seen a marked improvement in my health as I incorporate soy products into my diet. Research also shows that soy can be helpful in the fight against obesity.

Organic Butter: In recipes where only butter will do, you can buy organic, unsalted, hormone-free butter from most grocery stores.

Cheese: The cream cheeses that have been used in these recipes will allow you to continue to enjoy some of your favorite dessert recipes like soy cream, cheesecake, and frostings for cakes. Regular cream cheese has been associated with high fat and extra calories. I have used Neufchâtel cheese, which is a reduced-fat alternative to cream cheese. I have also used a nondairy cream cheese that has no dairy butterfat or cholesterol. Finally, I used fat-free cream cheese to help you support your healthy lifestyle.

EGGS

I am so "eggcited" to offer several recipes that are eggless. I use organic eggs or eggs from free-range hens, which are farmed without the use of hormones and pesticides. I also use egg substitutes when feasible. However, egg substitutes will not work for all recipes. When a cake recipe requires more than four eggs, the egg substitutes do not yield the desired results. However, they work very well in recipes for cookies, fruit breads, and puddings.

TOFU

Tofu, also known as soybean curd, is a soft, cheeselike food made by curdling fresh hot soymilk with a coagulant. Tofu is a bland product that easily absorbs the flavors of other ingredients with which it is cooked. Tofu is rich in high-quality protein and B-vitamins and low in sodium. Tofu is found in your local grocery store. There is shelf tofu and refrigerated tofu. Tofu is available in several textures: silken, soft, medium firm, and extra firm.

Firm tofu is dense and solid and can be cubed and served in soups, stir fried, or grilled. Firm tofu is higher in protein, fat, and calcium than other forms of tofu. Soft tofu is good for recipes that call for blended tofu. Silken tofu is a creamy product and can be used as a replacement for sour cream in many dip recipes. I use silken regular and low-fat tofu in my ice cream recipes.

Vegetable Shortening and Oil
I used to hear the word *fat* and just cringe. When fat-free and low-fat desserts hit the market, I thought I was home free. I bought every fat-free product on the market. Several years ago, I learned that most fat-free recipes contained two to three times the amount of sugar as regular recipes. In several of my recipes I have used low-fat products, but I reduced the amount of sugar.

I use organic butter and soy margarine and canola oil and vegetable shortening. I select the fat that will yield the best flavor and results. I have reduced the amount of fat that many of my traditional recipes required as much as possible.

CHOCOLATES AND CAROB

Some say chocolate was the beginning of sin, but I believe that it was the making of heaven. When I use chocolate in my recipes, I use unsweetened chocolates, natural semisweet chocolate, or unsweetened Dutch-processed cocoa. People who refrain from eating chocolate sometimes use carob as a substitute. The long, leathery pods from the tropical carob tree contain a sweet, edible pulp (that can be eaten fresh) and a few hard, inedible seeds. After drying, the pulp is roasted and ground into a powder. It is then used to flavor baked goods and candies. Both fresh and dried carob pods, as well as carob powder, may be found in health-food and specialty food stores. Because carob is sweet and tastes vaguely of chocolate, it's often used as a chocolate substitute.

OTHER SUBSTITUTIONS AND ADDITIONAL INGREDIENT INFORMATION

I hope my recipes will inspire you to try substituting healthy ingredients in some of your own favorite recipes. The list below represents ingredients used in the recipes in this book. However, this list is by no means complete. When you open your eyes to the ingredients called for in many recipes and spend some time experimenting with healthy alternatives, you'll soon see that you can have your cake and eat it, too.

Applesauce (Unsweetened): Unsweetened applesauce can be used to reduce oil in recipes.

Baking Powder: I only use aluminum-free baking powder.

Coconut: Only unsweetened coconut flakes are used in my recipes. I also use dried unsweetened coconut and frozen fresh unsweetened coconut.

Cookies and Crackers: I only use organic cookies and crackers when they are required in a recipe.

Extracts: I use natural and regular extract instead of imitation flavor in all of my recipes. You can also use nonalcoholic extracts.

Gelatins: When I am making dairy-free recipes that require gelatin, I use kosher gelatin. I also use an unsweetened store-brand gelatin in many of my recipes.

Peanut Butter: When a recipe requires peanut butter, make sure that it is natural, with no added sugar.

Rice: I use brown basmati rice to make rice pudding. However, there are some brands of white rice that are excellent substitutes. If you are more comfortable with white rice, check out the selection in the health food department of your grocery store.

Salt: I do not use regular salt. I only use iodized sea salt in my recipes.

Nutritional Information

Our *Dessert Lovers* nutrition team has prepared and analyzed all of the recipes in this book using the latest nutritional software and guidelines from the USDA and American Diabetic Association. We've provided nutritional information for most of the recipes in this collection, including: calories, carbohydrates, fiber, protein, fat, and sodium. We've also provided the number of servings per recipes and the size of servings in grams. We've chosen to represent serving sizes in grams because it is the most precise.

Please note that the listed gram value per serving refers only to the weight of the serving. This value is not the total of the individual nutrients.

All nutrient values are also given in grams except for sodium, which is given in milligrams. Most of the nutritional values have been rounded up to the nearest whole number if the value is .50 or greater. Fiber has been left in the original number of grams calculated for those who count fiber grams.

For example, our Luscious Creamy Cheesecake (page 56):

MAKES 18 SERVINGS, 86 GRAMS EACH
(the 86 represents only the weight of the serving measured in grams)

NUTRITIONAL INFORMATION PER SERVING:
Calories 244, Carbohydrates 20.5g, Fiber .75g, Sugar 13g, Protein 7g, Fat 15g, Sodium 282mg

Many of the recipes include low-fat or dairy-free versions, and we've included those nutritional values as well. In the Cakes section, I've listed the nutritional values for the cakes and frostings separately for those who may wish to just eat the cake alone. To get the nutritional value of the cake with frosting, simply add the values together. The same advice goes for any other recipe where you might add a topping as a variation. In the Cheesecakes section, for example, you might choose to add some of the fruit topping to any of the cheesecakes. Just be sure to add the nutritional value per serving of the topping to your serving of cheesecake.

NUTRITIONAL ICONS

Our *Dessert Lovers* nutrition team has developed the following icons in order to help you quickly identify recipes suited to your special dietary needs.

Diabetic-Friendly Recipes

Diabetes affects approximately sixteen million people in the United States. There are two types of diabetes: Type 1 and Type 2, both requiring medication and dietary lifestyle changes. In the past, because of their inability to metabolize sugar normally, diabetics were cautioned to limit or totally restrict consumption of sugars and starches. However, the current diet strategy is to control blood sugar by managing the overall carbohydrate, protein, and fat in the diet. *The American Dietetic Association's Complete Food and Nutrition Guide* notes that "Experts today recognize that sugar and starches have similar effects on blood sugar levels . . . the amount of carbohydrate, not the source is the issue. According to the American Diabetes Association, moderate amounts of sugar can be part of a well-balanced diet." Having diabetes doesn't necessarily mean you have to serve a life sentence of boring food. The recipes marked as diabetes-friendly contain 30 grams or less of carbohydrates and 10 grams or less of fat per serving. These amounts appear to be comparable, and the values are actually less than dessert recipes in other cookbooks for diabetics.

The recipes selected as diabetic-friendly by the *Dessert Lovers* nutrition team include a nutritional breakdown, as well as diabetic exchanges to help with meal planning. These recipes can be incorporated into a healthy diabetic meal plan, but it is important to understand your particular nutrition and medication needs. Consult your doctor or dietitian about any questions you may have.

LOW-FAT RECIPES

Over sixty million Americans go on some sort of diet or exercise plan each year, but we are still losing the battle of the bulge. More than 60 percent of the U.S. population is now considered to be overweight.

Reducing your daily caloric intake, eating a balanced diet, and increasing your activity are all proven ways to manage your weight. Avoiding sweets entirely is not. Most people are certainly capable of abstaining from fatty foods, chocolate, or sugary desserts, but only often for a limited time. Soon, our resolve weakens, and instead of treating ourselves to our favorite foods on occasion, we binge on them, damaging our health and creating feelings of doubt and failure at having given in to temptation.

There are over thirty recipes in this collection that meet the FDA's guidelines for being low-fat. This means that these recipes contain less than 3 grams of fat per serving. In addition, there are over twenty recipes that, although are not low-fat, are considered reduced fat since they contain 25 percent less fat per serving than the "original" food they are being compared to.

Look for the Low-Fat icon throughout this book to quickly identify those dishes that will reduce your calories-from-fat intake. Look for "On the Lighter Side" to quickly find lighter, reduced-fat versions of favorite recipes.

FOOD ALLERGIES

Nearly seven million Americans suffer from food allergies, and physicians report that this figure is on the rise.

The most common food allergens are: peanuts, tree nuts (walnuts, pecans, etc.), fish, shellfish, eggs, milk, soy, and wheat. Peanuts are the leading cause of severe allergic reactions, followed by shellfish, fish, tree nuts, and eggs.

If you have an allergy, or a family member with an allergy, you know how tiring it is to read labels, avoid packaged food, and have restaurant meals. For many who suffer with allergies, there is often a great sense of deprivation as they watch others eat with abandon. This deprivation is especially hard for children who often must eat special meals at school or have to bring their own treats to parties and gatherings.

Dessert Lovers' Choice has over seventy nut-free recipes, over seventy dairy-free recipes, and over sixty egg-free recipes that taste remarkable and will be loved by all.

But a word of caution: Although the recipes have been created and tested with allergen-free foods, it is always necessary to read labels to ensure that the ingredients you are using are completely allergen free. In the Cakes section, please note that many of the cake recipes are dairy-free, but the frosting you add may not be unless I've provided a dairy-free version.

A FINAL WORD

The recipes in this book are delicious and easy to make. You'll soon be able to enjoy the sweet smell of fresh cookies, the rich and creamy texture of frozen desserts, and even a birthday cake that taste good, look good, and are good for you. This collection also includes guilt-free cheesecakes and homey pies that are special enough for Sunday brunch but healthy enough to enjoy every day. Because only fresh or frozen ingredients are used, there are fewer preservatives, natural or artificial, in these recipes. As a result, I suggest that you prepare and enjoy these treats within a few days of preparation for maximum flavor, texture, and freshness. I hope that the recipes in this book will inspire you to rethink some of your favorite dishes and to experiment with organic products, soy, and natural sugars on your journey to a healthier lifestyle.

COOKIES

In kindergarten, my skill at marbles led to stacks of cookies. When I was five years old, I attended kindergarten in a two-room schoolhouse with several of my siblings. Although mom always prepared our lunches, we would still buy a Big Jack Cookie and a carton of chocolate milk at school. It was at that time that I learned to shoot marbles. The boys at school tried to keep me out of their "Steel Marble Club" because it was for boys only. It was, at least, until the captain, Charlie Brown, fell in love with me, and the club's rules began to change. I soon became an official member. The idea behind the game was to win the "steel marble."

It turns out I was better than most of those boys. I kept winning, and before long they were calling me "Keeper of the Steel Marbles." My bag of steel marbles was the envy of them all, and I soon discovered that the boys would do almost anything to get back their steel marbles. So I would trade most of my steel marbles for their Big Jack Cookies, and by lunchtime I would have at least a half dozen cookies. Life was very sweet indeed!

Though Big Jack Cookies hold a permanent place in my memory, the very first cookies I remember tasting were my mother's tea cake cookies. Let me tell you, you have not had a *real* cookie until you have had one of my mother's tea cakes! When I asked my mother how she made them, she told me that her mother and grandmother would sample a cake by testing several small portions of cake batter in a pan, resulting in small teacakes.

When I became a mother, many of the cookies I baked were made from store-bought cookie dough so that I would have more time to spend with my son. However, my love for cookies remained strong whether I was baking them or buying them. To create cookie recipes that were both tasty and healthier, I used ingredients with fiber and vitamins such as whole-grain and unbleached flour to support my new healthy lifestyle. The whole-grain flours are higher in fiber, which contain lots of vitamins *and* are very filling. Whole grain provides great texture to the recipes. I also used other natural ingredients such as soy milk, soy butter, and natural sugar to reduce calories and sugar. In this section, you'll find some excellent recipes for adults and children alike. I hope that you have as much fun baking them as I did creating them.

Schoolhouse Oatmeal Raisin Cookies

MAKES 24 SERVINGS, 40 GRAMS PER SERVING

1 cup all-purpose unbleached
white flour

½ cup pastry wheat flour or
½ cup oat flour

1 teaspoon baking soda

2 teaspoons ground cinnamon

½ teaspoon salt

¾ cup soy margarine

¾ cup natural sugar

2 organic eggs, or egg
substitute equivalent to
2 eggs

1 teaspoon vanilla extract

2 tablespoons applesauce

2 cups uncooked old-fashioned
oatmeal

¾ cup raisins

¾ cup finely chopped pecans,
optional

Preheat oven to 350 degrees. Combine flours, baking soda, cinnamon, and salt; set aside. Using an electric mixer on medium speed, cream vegetable oil and sugar. Add eggs, vanilla, and applesauce; mix well. Add flour mixture to sugar mixture and beat just until blended. Using a wooden spoon or rubber spatula, stir in oats, raisins, and pecans (if desired).

Lightly coat the inside of a standard ice cream scoop (one that holds 2 tablespoons) with cooking spray. Using scoop, drop dough onto an ungreased cookie sheet. Leave 2 inches between scoops of dough.

Bake 12 to 17 minutes or until lightly browned. Cool several minutes on cookie sheet before transferring cookies to wire rack to cool completely.

● **NUTRITIONAL INFORMATION PER SERVING:**
Calories 148, Carbohydrates 23g, Fiber 2g, Sugar 11g, Protein 4g, Fat 4g, Sodium 141mg
● **DIABETIC EXCHANGES:** 1½ Starch, ½ Fat

Chunky Chocolate Cookies

MAKES 24 SERVINGS, 38 GRAMS PER SERVING

Preheat oven to 375 degrees. Combine flours, baking soda, and salt in a medium bowl; set aside. Using an electric mixer on medium speed, cream margarine and sugar. Add egg and vanilla extract. Mix well. Gradually beat in flour mixture. Stir in chocolate bits and nuts with a wooden spoon or rubber spatula.

Lightly coat the inside of a standard ice cream scoop (holds 2 tablespoons) with cooking spray, and use the scoop to drop dough on an ungreased cookie sheet. Leave 2 inches between scoops of dough.

Bake 12 to 15 minutes or until lightly browned. Cool several minutes on cookie sheet.

- 1 cup all-purpose unbleached white flour
- ¾ cup oat flour
- ¾ teaspoon baking soda
- ¼ teaspoon salt
- ¾ cup soy margarine
- 1 cup natural sugar
- 1 organic egg
- 1 teaspoon vanilla extract
- 6 ounces semisweet chocolate chunks, broken into bits, or carob chips
- ¾ cup finely chopped pecans

● **NUTRITIONAL INFORMATION PER SERVING:**
Calories 175, Carbohydrates 22g, Fiber 2g, Sugar 13g, Protein 4g, Fat 9g, Sodium 99mg

● **DIABETIC EXCHANGES:** 1½ Starch, 1 Fat

Almond Biscotti

MAKES 36 SERVINGS, 18 GRAMS PER SERVING

1½ cups all-purpose unbleached white flour

½ cup oat flour

½ teaspoon baking powder

½ cup butter-flavored vegetable shortening

⅔ cup natural sugar

2 organic eggs, beaten

1 teaspoon almond extract

½ cup finely chopped almonds

These biscotti are prepared using unbleached and unbromated flour, natural sugar, and eggs. These ingredients yield a low-calorie, low-fat, and low-carbohydrate treat with only 80 calories per serving. Traditionally, biscotti were an after-dinner dessert or snack, but I recommend serving these biscotti with coffee, tea, espresso, hot chocolate, or soy milk any time, including for breakfast.

Preheat oven to 375 degrees. Lightly grease a cookie sheet with cooking spray and set aside. Sift flours and baking powder; set aside.

Using an electric mixer on medium speed, blend shortening and sugar until well-blended; add eggs and almond extract, and blend until mixture is creamy. Add flour mixture one-third at a time, beating well after each addition. Stir in chopped almonds with a wooden spoon or rubber spatula.

Shape dough and divide it equally in half. Roll each piece into a 9-inch log. Press each log until it expands to about 2 inches in width, and place 3 inches apart on prepared cookie sheet. Bake for 25 minutes. Remove from oven.

When logs have cooled enough to handle, cut them into ½-inch-thick slices crosswise. Place slices on baking sheet and bake for 10 minutes. Remove from oven and use a spatula to turn the slices. Return to the oven and bake for an additional 5 minutes. Cool biscotti slices on wire racks.

● **NUTRITIONAL INFORMATION PER SERVING:**
Calories 77, Carbohydrates 9g, Fiber .35g, Sugar 4g, Protein 2g, Fat 4g, Sodium 9mg

● **DIABETIC EXCHANGES:** 1 Starch

Southern Pecan Biscotti

MAKES 36 SERVINGS, 18 GRAMS PER SERVING

Preheat oven to 375 degrees. Lightly grease cookie sheet with cooking spray and set aside. Sift flours and baking powder; set aside.

With a mixer on medium speed, blend shortening and sugar until well-blended; add eggs and vanilla extract. Add sifted flour mixture by the spoonful, beating well after each addition. Stir in chopped pecans with a wooden spoon or rubber spatula.

Shape dough and divide it equally in half. Roll each piece into a 9-inch log. Press each log until it expands to about 2 inches in width, and place 3 inches apart on prepared cookie sheet. Bake for 25 minutes. Remove from oven.

When logs have cooled enough to handle, cut into ½-inch-thick slices crosswise. Place slices on cookie sheet, and bake for 10 minutes. Remove from oven and use a spatula to turn the slices. Return to oven and bake for an additional 5 minutes. Cool biscotti slices on wire racks.

1¼ cups all-purpose unbleached white flour
¾ cup oat flour
1 teaspoon baking powder
½ cup buttered-flavored vegetable shortening
⅔ cup natural sugar
2 organic eggs or egg substitute equivalent to 2 eggs
2 teaspoons vanilla extract
½ cup finely chopped pecans

● **NUTRITIONAL INFORMATION PER SERVING:**
Calories 79, Carbohydrates 9g, Fiber .41g, Sugar 4g, Protein 1g, Fat 4g, Sodium 15mg
● **DIABETIC EXCHANGES:** 1 Starch

Sugar Cookies

¾ cup vegetable shortening

¾ cup plus 2 tablespoons
    natural sugar

2 organic eggs

1 teaspoon vanilla extract

1⅓ cup all-purpose unbleached
    white flour

¼ teaspoon salt (optional)

Preheat oven to 375 degrees. Using an electric mixer on medium speed, beat shortening for 30 seconds. Add ¾ cup sugar; beat until combined. Beat in eggs and vanilla.

Gradually mix in flour using mixer until batter becomes stiff. Switch to a wooden spoon to stir in remaining flour. Add salt (if desired).

Shape dough into 1-inch balls. Roll balls in remaining 2 tablespoons sugar before placing them 2 inches apart on an ungreased cookie sheet. Bake for 7 to 8 minutes or until lightly browned. Transfer cookies to a wire rack to cool.

• **NUTRITIONAL INFORMATION PER SERVING:**
Calories 117, Carbohydrates 13g, Fiber 0g, Sugar 7g, Protein 1g, Fat 7g, Sodium 5mg
• **DIABETIC EXCHANGES:** 1 Starch, 1 Fat

Better Than Fudge Brownies

MAKES 24 SERVINGS, 30 GRAMS PER SERVING

Preheat oven to 350 degrees. Prepare a 13x9x2-inch baking dish with cooking spray and set aside. Sift together flours, baking soda, and cocoa powder; set aside.

Combine sugar and margarine and chocolate in a medium bowl. Use whisk to blend in half of the eggs into the chocolate mixture. Whisk until the mixture begins to become creamy, then add the remainder of the eggs and whisk until creamy. Add extracts and water and whisk until mixture is smooth. Gradually add sifted flour mixture. Stir in nuts with a wooden spoon or rubber spatula. Spread mixture into prepared baking pan.

Bake for 20 minutes. Allow brownies to cool in pan before cutting into squares.

- **NUTRITIONAL INFORMATION PER SERVING:**
Calories 117, Carbohydrates 17g, Fiber 1g, Sugar 9g, Protein 3g, Fat 5g, Sodium 41mg
- **DIABETIC EXCHANGES:** 1 Starch, 1 Fat

1 cup unbleached all-purpose white flour

⅓ cup oat or wheat flour

¼ teaspoon baking soda

1 tablespoon Dutch-processed cocoa powder

1 cup natural sugar

½ cup soy margarine

3 (1 oz.) squares chocolate, melted

2 organic eggs, beaten

2 teaspoons vanilla extract

½ teaspoon lemon extract

⅛ cup water

⅓ cup walnuts, chopped (optional)

Tea Cakes

3 cups all-purpose unbleached
white flour

2 teaspoons baking powder

1 teaspoon nutmeg

½ teaspoon cinnamon

½ cup soy margarine

1 cup sugar

2 organic eggs, beaten

2 teaspoons vanilla extract

2 tablespoons soy milk

This is an old-fashioned, no-fuss recipe that was handed down through our family from my great-grandmother. I have modified the recipe by using more natural ingredients such as unbleached flour, natural sugar, soy margarine, soy milk, and organic eggs. This recipe can be prepared quickly and baked even quicker. It is absolutely great served with tea or milk.

Preheat oven to 375 degrees. In a medium bowl mix flour, baking powder, nutmeg, and cinnamon. Cut the soy margarine into the flour mixture until it resembles coarse crumbs; set aside.

Using a mixer on medium speed, mix sugar, eggs, vanilla, and milk. Gradually blend in flour mixture one large spoonful at a time.

Drop dough by rounded teaspoons 2 inches apart on an ungreased cookie sheet. Bake 8 to 10 minutes or until edges begin to brown. Cool on cookie sheet for several minutes before transferring to a wire rack to cool completely.

● **NUTRITIONAL INFORMATION PER SERVING:**
Calories 132, Carbohydrates 23g, Fiber .46g, Sugar 9g, Protein 4g, Fat 3g, Sodium 61mg
● **DIABETIC EXCHANGES:** 1½ Starch, ½ Fat

Better-Than-Butter Cookies

MAKES 24 SERVINGS, 43 GRAMS PER SERVING

Preheat oven to 350 degrees. Prepare a cookie sheet with cooking spray; set aside. Sift flour, baking powder, baking soda, and salt (if desired); set aside.

Using an electric mixer on medium speed, blend margarine, sugar, eggs, sour cream, soy milk, and vanilla extract until creamy. Gradually blend in flour mixture. Stir in walnuts with a wooden spoon or rubber spatula.

Drop dough by rounded teaspoons 2 inches apart on prepared cookie sheet. Bake approximately 10 minutes or until edges begin to brown. Transfer cookies to a wire rack to cool.

- **NUTRITIONAL INFORMATION PER SERVING:**
Calories 153, Carbohydrates 19g, Fiber .67g, Sugar 6g, Protein 4g, Fat 7g, Sodium 93mg
- **DIABETIC EXCHANGES:** 1½ Starch, 1 Fat

2½ cups all-purpose unbleached white flour
1 teaspoon baking soda
½ teaspoon baking powder
¼ teaspoon salt (optional)
½ cup soy margarine or organic butter
⅔ cup natural sugar
2 organic eggs, beaten
1 (8-oz.) carton sour cream
2 teaspoons soy milk
1 teaspoon vanilla extract
¾ cup walnuts, chopped

Peanut Butter Cookies

½ cup organic soy margarine

½ cup natural peanut butter

¾ cup natural sugar

½ teaspoon baking powder

1 teaspoon baking soda

2 organic eggs, or egg
   substitute equivalent to
   2 eggs

1 teaspoon vanilla extract

1 cup all-purpose unbleached
   white flour

¼ cup wheat pastry flour

Preheat oven to 375 degrees. Using an electric mixer on medium speed, beat margarine and peanut butter for 30 seconds. Add sugar, baking powder, and baking soda. Beat well, stopping mixer to scrape sides of bowl as necessary. Beat in eggs and vanilla extract until well-blended.

Sift flours together, then beat in as much of the flour as the mixer can handle. Use a wooden spoon or rubber spatula to stir in any remaining flour. Cover and chill dough approximately 30 minutes.

Roll dough into 1-inch balls. Arrange balls 2 inches apart on an ungreased cookie sheet. Flatten by making crisscross marks with the tines of a fork. Bake for 7 to 9 minutes or until bottoms are lightly browned. Transfer cookies to a wire rack to cool.

● **NUTRITIONAL INFORMATION PER SERVING:**
Calories 118, Carbohydrates 15g, Fiber 1g, Sugar 7g, Protein 4g, Fat 5g, Sodium 113mg
● **DIABETIC EXCHANGES:** 1 Starch, 1 Fat

'Tis the Season Cookies

MAKES 24 SERVINGS, 26 GRAMS PER SERVING

These cookies are a great choice for the holidays.

Preheat oven to 350 degrees. Using an electric mixer on medium speed, cream shortening and sugar. Blend in egg and vanilla extract. Stir in chopped almonds with a rubber spoon or wooden spatula. Gradually add flour by the spoonful to the creamed mixture. Cover and refrigerate dough for 30 minutes.

Form dough into 1-inch balls and place them 2 inches apart on an ungreased cookie sheet. Indent the dough using the back of a measuring teaspoon. Place a small dab of jelly into each indentation.

Bake cookies for 12 to 15 minutes. Remove from oven; let cookies cool for several minutes on the cookie sheet before transferring to a wire rack to cool.

½ cup vegetable shortening
¼ cup natural sugar
1 organic egg, beaten
1 teaspoon vanilla extract
½ cup chopped almonds or pecans
1 cup unbleached all-purpose white flour
¾ cup natural strawberry jelly

• **NUTRITIONAL INFORMATION PER SERVING:**
Calories 107, Carbohydrates 13g, Fiber .27g, Sugar 8g, Protein 1g, Fat 5g, Sodium 3mg
• **DIABETIC EXCHANGES:** 1 Starch, ½ Fat

CAKES

The Timeless Aroma of Mom's Sweet Bread

My first memory of cakes is of my mom's sweet bread. I always knew when she was going to make sweet bread because she would take out her ingredients the day before she baked. The next day, I would watch her carefully place all the ingredients in a small, worn bowl, and I have no memory of her ever using a measuring cup or measuring spoon. After my mother quickly mixed all of the ingredients, she allowed me to sample the batter before she poured the mixture into an old, beaten, tin cake pan. Then she would place the pan in a big, wood-burning, black-belly stove.

Mom normally made only one pan of sweet bread, but if we were expecting company, she made two pans. Since she only had one pan for baking cakes, she would wash the pan and reuse it to get her second pan of sweet bread. I always knew when the cake was ready because the sweet aroma wafted through every corner of our three-room house when Mom removed the cake from the stove and set it on top to cool.

It was called sweet bread, rather than cake, because the recipe only called for self-rising white flour, homemade butter, eggs (which we got from the henhouse), sugar, vanilla flavor, and canned milk. She used fewer eggs than when she made a layer cake, and she never frosted her sweet bread. Mom only frosted cakes for special occasions like Easter or Christmas. At such times, my mother made several specialty cakes such as caramel cake, coconut cake, and chocolate cake. These were the cakes that Santa liked most. But to her kids, all of Mom's cakes were special.

Today, my baking approach incorporates the techniques and skills of my mother and my ancestors, whom I have admired and respected over the years. It has also embraced the techniques and skills of those who have introduced me to tasty, nontraditional desserts from the vegetarian community.

I selected flours that were milled in such a way that they are high in protein, which results in greater moisture retention necessary for my cakes. I have substituted whole grain flour for enriched bleached flours. In addition to being highly nutritional, they are also high in fiber. They also yield great taste and texture. Oil and fat were reduced to a minimum. I substituted soy margarine and vegetable oil, which greatly reduced the saturated fat in my recipes without sacrificing the flavor and rich taste.

Heavenly Chocolate Cake

MAKES 18 SERVINGS, 83 GRAMS PER SERVING

1½ cups unbleached, all-purpose white flour

1 cup oat flour

1½ cups natural sugar

½ cup Dutch-processed cocoa

1½ teaspoons baking powder

1 teaspoon baking soda

½ cup soy milk

1 tablespoon apple cider vinegar

2 teaspoons vanilla extract

1 teaspoon lemon extract

1 cup cold water

4 organic eggs

1 cup soy margarine, melted

Preheat oven to 350 degrees. Grease and flour two 9-inch cake pans; set aside. Sift flours together, then add sugar, cocoa, baking powder, and baking soda and sift again; set aside.

Using a wire whisk, mix together soy milk, vinegar, vanilla extract, lemon extract, and water in a separate bowl. Add eggs, one at a time, beating well after each addition. Add melted margarine, whisking to blend well. Pour egg mixture over sifted dry ingredients. Whisk ingredients into a smooth batter. Immediately spoon batter into pans.

Bake for 35 to 40 minutes or until a wooden toothpick inserted in the center of each layer comes out clean. Place the pans on a wire rack to cool. Use either Heavenly Chocolate Frosting (page 30) or Chocolate Supreme Cream Cheese Frosting (page 31), if desired.

Cover top of bottom layer with frosting. Place second layer on top, then cover both layers completely with frosting.

● **NUTRITIONAL INFORMATION PER SERVING:**
Calories 238, Carbohydrates 35g, Fiber 3g, Sugar 18g, Protein 7g, Fat 8g, Sodium 178mg

Eggless Heavenly Chocolate Cake

MAKES 18 SERVINGS, 79 GRAMS PER SERVING

This recipe was created as a lower-calorie version of my Heavenly Chocolate Cake for those who love chocolate cake but who need to watch calories, fat, and carbohydrates, or for those who have removed eggs from their diet. It can be served with or without frosting. If using frosting, I recommend the Chocolate Supreme Nondairy Cream Cheese Frosting.

1½ cups all-purpose unbleached white flour

1 cup oat flour

1½ cups natural sugar

½ cup Dutch-processed cocoa

1 teaspoon baking powder

2 teaspoons baking soda

2 tablespoons apple cider vinegar

2 teaspoons vanilla extract

1 teaspoon lemon extract

1 cup cold water

1 cup soy milk

1 cup soy margarine, melted

Preheat oven to 350 degrees. Grease and flour two 9-inch cake pans; set aside. Sift flours together, then add sugar, cocoa, baking powder, and baking soda and sift again; set aside.

Whisk together vinegar, vanilla extract, lemon extract, water, and soy milk. Add melted margarine, whisking to blend well. Pour margarine mixture over sifted dry ingredients. Use the whisk to blend ingredients into a smooth batter. Immediately spoon batter into pans.

Bake for 35 to 40 minutes or until a wooden toothpick inserted in the center of each layer comes out clean. Place pans on a wire rack to cool. Use Chocolate Supreme Nondairy Cream Cheese Frosting (page 31), if desired.

● NUTRITIONAL INFORMATION PER SERVING:
Calories 224, Carbohydrates 35g, Fiber 3g, Sugar 17g, Protein 6g, Fat 7g, Sodium 224mg

Heavenly Chocolate Frosting

MAKES 18 SERVINGS, 26 GRAMS PER SERVING

⅔ cup Dutch-processed cocoa

¾ cup natural sugar

½ cup unsalted organic butter, melted

½ cup soy milk

1 teaspoon lemon extract

2 teaspoons vanilla extract

Mix cocoa and sugar; melt butter and stir into mixture. Warm soy milk gently, then add it along with lemon extract and vanilla extract to cocoa mixture.

Using an electric mixer on medium speed, blend until smooth. Cover top of bottom layer with frosting. Place second layer on top, the cover both layers completely with frosting.

● **NUTRITIONAL INFORMATION PER SERVING:**

Calories 90, Carbohydrates 13g, Fiber 1g, Sugar 9g, Protein 2g, Fat 3g, Sodium 30mg

Chocolate Supreme Cream Cheese Frosting

MAKES 18 SERVINGS, 37 GRAMS PER SERVING

Using an electric mixer on medium speed, blend cream cheese and margarine. Mix cocoa and sugar together and then blend into the cream cheese mixture. Add vanilla extract. Cover top of bottom layer with frosting. Place second layer on top, then cover both layers completely with frosting.

16 ounces Neufchâtel cheese
1 tablespoon soy margarine
½ cup Dutch-processed cocoa powder
¾ cup natural sugar
2 teaspoons vanilla extract

● **NUTRITIONAL INFORMATION PER SERVING:**
Calories 113, Carbohydrates 11g, Fiber .70g, Sugar 9g, Protein 3g, Fat 6g, Sodium 105mg

Variations:

Low-Fat

MAKES 18 SERVINGS, 37 GRAMS PER SERVING

Substitute 16 ounces fat-free cream cheese for Neufchâtel cheese.

● **NUTRITIONAL INFORMATION PER SERVING:**
Calories 72, Carbohydrates 11g, Fiber .70g, Sugar 8g, Protein 4g, Fat 1g, Sodium 141mg

Dairy-Free

MAKES 18 SERVINGS, 37 GRAMS PER SERVING

Substitute 16 ounces nondairy cream cheese for Neufchâtel cheese.

● **NUTRITIONAL INFORMATION PER SERVING:**
Calories 92, Carbohydrates 12g, Fiber 0g, Sugar 8g, Protein 34g, Fat 3g, Sodium 200mg

Old-Fashioned Buttermilk Pound Cake

MAKES 16 SERVINGS, 91 GRAMS PER SERVING

½ cup soy margarine chilled
    45 minutes in freezer

½ cup vegetable shortening

1¼ cups natural sugar

½ cup unsweetened
    applesauce

5 organic eggs

2 teaspoons white vinegar

1 cup soy milk

⅛ teaspoon baking soda

2½ cups all-purpose
    unbleached white flour

⅛ teaspoon sea salt

2 teaspoons vanilla extract

1 teaspoon almond extract

Preheat oven to 350 degrees. Grease and flour a 10-inch Bundt pan; set aside.

Using an electric mixture on low speed, cream together chilled margarine and vegetable shortening; gradually add sugar, beating well on medium speed. Add applesauce and eggs one at a time, beating well after each addition.

In a separate bowl, combine vinegar and soy milk. Dissolve baking soda in mixture; set aside. Sift flour and salt together. Gradually add flour mixture to creamed ingredients alternately with soy milk mixture, beginning and ending with flour mixture. Stir in vanilla extract and almond extract.

Pour batter into prepared pan and bake for 40 to 50 minutes or until a wooden toothpick inserted in the middle comes out clean. Place pan on a wire rack to cool.

● **NUTRITIONAL INFORMATION PER SERVING:**
Calories 272, Carbohydrates 36g, Fiber 1g, Sugar 17g, Protein 6g, Fat 11g, Sodium 83mg

Carrot Cake

MAKES 18 SERVINGS, 86 GRAMS PER SERVING

Preheat oven to 350 degrees. Grease and flour two 9-inch cake pans; set aside.

Sift together flour, baking powder, baking soda, cinnamon, sugar, and salt, if desired; set aside.

Use a whisk to beat eggs until frothy. Blend in vanilla extract and water. Slowly pour in oil and whisk until mixture is well-combined. Pour carrots and crushed nuts on top of sifted flour mixture; do not stir. Spoon egg mixture over flour and carrots. Use the whisk to blend ingredients into a smooth batter. Immediately spoon batter into pans.

Bake for 35 to 40 minutes or until a wooden toothpick inserted into the center of each layer comes out clean. Place pans on a wire rack to cool. Cover with Vanilla Cream Cheese Frosting (page 34).

2½ cups all-purpose unbleached organic white flour
2 teaspoons baking powder
1 teaspoon baking soda
2 teaspoons cinnamon
1½ cups natural sugar
1 teaspoon salt, optional
4 organic eggs
2 teaspoons vanilla extract
½ cup water
¾ cup canola oil
3 cups grated carrots
½ cup crushed walnuts

• NUTRITIONAL INFORMATION PER SERVING:
Calories 263, Carbohydrates 33g, Fiber 1g, Sugar 18g, Protein 4g, Fat 13g, Sodium 135mg

Vanilla Cream Cheese Frosting

MAKES 18 SERVINGS, 44 GRAMS PER SERVING

16 ounces Neufchâtel cheese

1 tablespoon soy margarine

¾ cup natural sugar

2 teaspoons vanilla extract

1 cup grated carrots

½ cup crushed walnuts

Using an electric mixer on low speed, blend cheese and margarine. Add sugar and vanilla extract, mixing until sugar dissolves. Cover top of bottom layer with frosting. Place second layer on top, then cover both layers completely with frosting. Sprinkle nuts and carrots on top of frosting for garnish.

• **NUTRITIONAL INFORMATION PER SERVING:**

Calories 129, Carbohydrates 11g, Fiber .48g, Sugar 9g, Protein 3g, Fat 8g, Sodium 107mg

• **DIABETIC EXCHANGES** 1 Carbohydrate, 1 Fat

Variations:

Low-Fat

MAKES 18 SERVINGS, 44 GRAMS PER SERVING

Substitute 16 ounces fat-free cream cheese for Neufchâtel cheese.

• **NUTRITIONAL INFORMATION PER SERVING:**
Calories 87, Carbohydrates 11g, Fiber .48g, Sugar 9g, Protein 4g, Fat 3g, Sodium 143mg
• **DIABETIC EXCHANGE:** 1 Carbohydrate

Dairy-Free

MAKES 18 SERVINGS, 44 GRAMS PER SERVING

Substitute 16 ounces nondairy cream cheese for Neufchâtel cheese.

• **NUTRITIONAL INFORMATION PER SERVING:**
Calories 108, Carbohydrates 12g, Fiber .48g, Sugar 9g, Protein 3g, Fat 5g, Sodium 202mg
• **DIABETIC EXCHANGES:** 1 Carbohydrate, 1 Fat

Red Velvet Cake

MAKES 16 SERVINGS, 75 GRAMS PER SERVING

Preheat oven to 350 degrees. Grease and flour two 9-inch cake pans; set aside.

In a small bowl, combine cocoa and natural food coloring; set aside. Sift together flours and salt; set aside. In a separate bowl, stir vinegar and baking soda into soy milk; set aside.

Using a mixer on medium speed, cream oil, sugar, and eggs until fluffy. Add cocoa to batter. Mix in sifted flour, alternating with soy milk mixture. Add applesauce, vanilla extract, and almond extract. Divide batter evenly among prepared pans.

Bake for 30 to 40 minutes or until a wooden toothpick inserted near center of each layer comes out clean. Cover with Cream Cheese Frosting (page 36).

● **NUTRITIONAL INFORMATION PER SERVING:**
Calories 228, Carbohydrates 34g, Fiber 1g, Sugar 18g, Protein 4g, Fat 8g, Sodium 125mg

4 tablespoons Dutch-processed cocoa

2 (1-oz.) bottles natural red food coloring

2 cups all-purpose unbleached white flour

½ cup wheat pastry flour or oat flour

¼ teaspoon salt

1 tablespoon white vinegar

1 teaspoon baking soda

1 cup soy milk

½ cup vegetable oil

1½ cups natural sugar

2 organic eggs

1 tablespoon unsweetened applesauce

1 teaspoon vanilla extract

1 teaspoon almond extract

Cream Cheese Frosting

MAKES 16 SERVINGS, 36 GRAMS PER SERVING

16 ounces Neufchâtel
  cream cheese
½ cup natural sugar
1 tablespoon soy margarine
2 teaspoons vanilla extract

Using an electric mixer on medium speed, combine all ingredients until smooth and creamy. Cover top of bottom layer with frosting. Place second layer on top, then cover both layers completely with frosting.

● **NUTRITIONAL INFORMATION PER SERVING:**
Calories 105, Carbohydrates 8g, Fiber 0g, Sugar 7g, Protein 3g, Fat 7g, Sodium 117mg

Variations:

Low-Fat

MAKES 16 SERVINGS, 36 GRAMS PER SERVING

Substitute 16 ounces fat-free cream cheese for Neufchâtel cheese.

● **NUTRITIONAL INFORMATION PER SERVING:**
Calories 59, Carbohydrates 8g, Fiber 0g, Sugar 6g, Protein 4g, Fat 1.0g, Sodium 159mg

Dairy-Free

MAKES 16 SERVINGS, 36 GRAMS PER SERVING

Substitute 16 ounces nondairy cream cheese for Neufchâtel cheese.

● **NUTRITIONAL INFORMATION PER SERVING:**
Calories 82, Carbohydrates 9g, Fiber 0g, Sugar 6g, Protein 2g, Fat 3g, Sodium 224mg

Pineapple Coconut Cake

MAKES 16 SERVINGS, 83 GRAMS PER SERVING WITH FROSTING

Preheat oven to 350 degrees. Grease and flour two 9-inch cake pans; set aside.

In a medium bowl, sift flour, baking powder, and salt (if desired); set aside. Using an electric mixer on medium speed, cream shortening and sugar; beat well. Add eggs, one at a time, beating after each addition. Gradually mix in flour mixture alternately with soy milk, beginning and ending with flour mixture. Stir in pineapple, coconut extract, and almond extract with a wooden spoon or rubber spatula.

Pour batter into pans. Bake for 25 to 30 minutes or until a wooden toothpick inserted in the center of each layer comes out clean. Remove pans from oven; run a dull dinner knife around sides to prevent sticking. Place pans on a wire rack to cool.

Cover each layer with Pineapple Coconut Frosting (page 38).

2½ cups all-purpose unbleached white flour

2 teaspoons baking powder

¾ teaspoon salt (optional)

¾ cup vegetable shortening

1 cup natural sugar

4 organic eggs

1 cup soy milk

¾ cup unsweetened crushed pineapple, drained

2 teaspoons coconut extract

1 teaspoon almond extract

● **NUTRITIONAL INFORMATION PER SERVING:**

Calories 239, Carbohydrates 30g, Fiber .29g, Sugar 14g, Protein 4g, Fat 11g, Sodium 69mg

Pineapple Coconut Frosting

MAKES 16 SERVINGS, 47 GRAMS PER SERVING

16 ounces Neufchâtel cheese

1 tablespoon soy margarine

½ cup natural sugar

½ cup unsweetened coconut flakes, fresh or frozen

½ cup unsweetened crushed pineapple, drained

Using an electric mixer on low speed, blend cheese and margarine; add sugar and coconut. Continue beating until light and fluffy. Mix in pineapple with a wooden spoon or rubber spatula. Cover top of bottom layer with frosting. Place second layer on top, then cover both layers completely with frosting.

● **NUTRITIONAL INFORMATION PER SERVING:**
Calories 126, Carbohydrates 10g, Fiber .39g, Sugar 9g, Protein 3g, Fat 8g, Sodium 129mg

Variations:

Low-Fat

MAKES 16 SERVINGS, 47 GRAMS PER SERVING

Substitute 16 ounces fat-free cream cheese for Neufchâtel cheese.

● **NUTRITIONAL INFORMATION PER SERVING:**
Calories 79, Carbohydrates 11g, Fiber .39g, Sugar 8g, Protein 5g, Fat 2g, Sodium 171mg

Dairy-Free

MAKES 16 SERVINGS, 47 GRAMS PER SERVING

Substitute 16 ounces nondairy cream cheese for Neufchâtel cheese.

● **NUTRITIONAL INFORMATION PER SERVING:**
Calories 102, Carbohydrates 11g, Fiber .39g, Sugar 8g, Protein 2g, Fat 5g, Sodium 236mg

Cinnamon Pecan Coffee Cake

MAKES 16 SERVINGS, 64 GRAMS PER SERVING

Preheat oven to 350 degrees. Grease and flour a 10-inch Bundt pan.

Combine ¼ cup sugar, cinnamon, and chopped pecans in a small bowl; set aside. Sift flours, baking powder, baking soda, and salt; set aside.

Using an electric mixer on medium speed, blend soy margarine and remaining ¾ cup sugar until light and fluffy. Beat in applesauce. Add eggs one at a time, beating well after each addition. Add almond extract. Spoon flour mixture into batter, alternating with sour cream and ending with flour mixture, and mix well.

Spoon half of the batter into the Bundt pan. Sprinkle pecan mixture over batter. Use a dinner knife to lightly swirl pecans through batter. Pour in remaining batter.

Bake at 350 degrees for 50 minutes or until a wooden toothpick inserted in the center comes out clean.

1 cup natural sugar, divided
2 teaspoons ground cinnamon
⅓ cup pecans, chopped
1½ cups all-purpose
    unbleached white flour
½ cup whole wheat pastry flour
1 teaspoon baking powder
1 teaspoon baking soda
½ teaspoon salt
½ cup soy margarine
2 tablespoons unsweetened
    applesauce
2 organic eggs
1 teaspoon almond extract
8 ounces nondairy sour cream
    substitute

• **NUTRITIONAL INFORMATION PER SERVING:**
Calories 209, Carbohydrates 29g, Sugar 13g, Fiber .2.0, Protein 5g, Fat 8g, Sodium 278mg

• **DIABETIC EXCHANGES:** Starch 2, Fat 1

Variation:

On the Lighter Side

MAKES 16 SERVINGS, 65 GRAMS PER SERVING

Substitute 8 ounces fat-free sour cream.

• **NUTRITIONAL INFORMATION PER SERVING:**
Calories 191, Carbohydrates 31g, Fiber 2g, Sugar 14g, Protein 5g, Fat 5g, Sodium 236mg

Lemon Poppy Seed Cake

8 ounces Neufchâtel cheese

6 organic eggs

2½ cups unbleached all-
purpose flour

1 teaspoon baking powder

1 teaspoon baking soda

¼ teaspoon salt

¾ cup soy margarine, melted

1½ cups natural sugar

2 tablespoons poppy seeds

2 teaspoons lemon extract

Preheat oven to 325 degrees. Allow cream cheese and eggs to stand at room temperature for 30 minutes. Grease and flour a 10-inch Bundt pan; set aside. Sift together flour, baking powder, baking soda, and salt; set aside.

Using an electric mixer on medium speed, beat soy margarine and cheese until creamy. Gradually add sugar, 2 tablespoons at a time, beating after each addition.

Continue beating until batter is light and fluffy. Mix in poppy seeds and lemon extract. With the mixer on low speed, add eggs, one at a time, beating for a moment after each addition. Scrape the bowl frequently. Keeping the mixer on low speed, slowly add flour mixture, mixing just enough to combine.

Pour batter into Bundt pan. Bake for 50 minutes or until a wooden toothpick inserted in the center of the pan comes out clean. Place pan on a wire rack to cool.

● **NUTRITIONAL INFORMATION PER SERVING:**
Calories 290, Carbohydrates 40g, Fiber 1g, Sugar 20g, Protein 9g, Fat 11g, Sodium 192mg

Variations:

On the Lighter Side

MAKES 16 SERVINGS, 87 GRAMS PER SERVING

Substitute 8 ounces fat-free cream cheese for the Neufchâtel cheese.

● **NUTRITIONAL INFORMATION PER SERVING:**
Calories 267, Carbohydrates 40g, Fiber 1g, Sugar 19g, Protein 9g, Fat 7g, Sodium 212mg

Dairy-Free

MAKES 16 SERVINGS, 87 GRAMS PER SERVING

Substitute 8 ounces nondairy cream cheese for the Neufchâtel cheese.

● **NUTRITIONAL INFORMATION PER SERVING:**
Calories 278, Carbohydrates 40g, Fiber 1g, Sugar 19g, Protein 8g, Fat 9g, Sodium 245mg

Simply Sweet Bread

MAKES 12 SERVINGS, 55 GRAMS PER SERVING

This recipe was adapted and modified from a recipe of my mother's. She called it "sweet bread." It is a plain layer cake without icing for a quick dessert. When the ingredients ran low for a fancy cake there was always flour, eggs, milk, butter, and vanilla flavor to whip up this simple cake. I have modified Mom's recipe with a reduced amount of natural sugar, soy margarine, eggs, vanilla extract, flour, and soy milk.

½ cup soy margarine

¾ cup natural sugar

2 organic eggs

2 teaspoons vanilla extract

1½ cup self-rising flour

⅓ cup soy milk

Preheat oven to 350 degrees. Grease and flour one 9-inch cake pan; set aside.

Use a mixer set on medium speed to blend soy margarine and sugar. Add eggs to margarine mixture one at a time, blending well before adding another. Add vanilla extract; beat well. Gradually add flour alternately with soy milk, beginning and ending with flour, and mix well.

Pour batter into prepared pan and bake for 30 minutes or until a wooden toothpick inserted in the center of cake comes out clean. Place pan on a wire rack to cool.

● **NUTRITIONAL INFORMATION PER SERVING:**

Calories 182, Carbohydrates 28g, Fiber 1g, Sugar 13g, Protein 5g, Fat 5g, Sodium 254mg

Sweet Molasses Bread

1½ cups all-purpose
   unbleached white flour
½ cup oat flour
1 teaspoon cinnamon
1 teaspoon baking powder
1 teaspoon baking soda
½ cup vegetable shortening
¾ cup natural sugar
2 organic eggs
⅓ cup raw molasses
1 teaspoon vanilla extract
½ cup water

MAKES 12 SERVINGS, 70 GRAMS PER SERVING

This sweet molasses bread goes well with hot tea or cold soy milk sprinkled with cinnamon.

Preheat oven to 350 degrees. Grease and flour a 6x11-inch loaf pan; set aside. Sift together flours, cinnamon, baking powder, and baking soda; set aside.

Using an electric mixer on medium speed, blend shortening and sugar until light and creamy. Add eggs, one at a time, beating after each addition. Blend in molasses and vanilla extract. Add flour mixture alternately with water, and mix well.

Spoon batter into loaf pan. Bake for 40 to 45 minutes or until a wooden toothpick inserted in the center comes out clean.

● **NUTRITIONAL INFORMATION PER SERVING:**
Calories 236, Carbohydrates 34g, Fiber .61g, Sugar 18g,
Protein 4g, Fat 9g, Sodium 153mg

Hummingbird Cake

MAKES 18 SERVINGS, 95 GRAMS PER SERVING

Preheat oven to 350 degrees. Grease and flour three 9-inch cake pans; set aside. Sift together flour, cinnamon, nutmeg, baking soda, and salt; set aside.

Using an electric mixer on medium speed, cream soy margarine and sugar. Add eggs one at a time, beating well after each addition. Blend in dry ingredients. Fold in mashed bananas, pineapple, vanilla extract, and pecans with a wooden spoon or rubber spatula.

Pour batter into pans. Bake for 30 minutes, or until a wooden toothpick inserted in center of each layer comes out clean. Place pans on a wire rack to cool.

• **NUTRITIONAL INFORMATION PER SERVING:**
Calories 262, Carbohydrates 39g, Fiber 2.4g, Sugar 18g, Protein 7g, Fat 9g, Sodium 190mg

2½ cups all-purpose unbleached white flour
½ cup wheat or oat flour
1 teaspoon ground cinnamon
1 teaspoon ground nutmeg
1 teaspoon baking soda
½ teaspoon salt
¾ cup soy margarine or vegetable oil
1 cup natural sugar
3 organic eggs
2 cups ripe bananas, mashed
8 ounces unsweetened crushed pineapple, including juice
2 teaspoons vanilla extract
¾ cup chopped pecans

Hummingbird Cake
Cream Cheese Frosting

MAKES 18 SERVINGS, 37 GRAMS PER SERVING

16 ounces Neufchâtel cheese
¼ cup vegetable oil
¾ cup natural sugar
2 teaspoon vanilla

Using an electric mixer on medium speed, blend all ingredients until creamy.

• **NUTRITIONAL INFORMATION PER SERVING:**
Calories 127, Carbohydrates 9g, Fiber 0g, Sugar 9g, Protein 3g, Fat 9g, Sodium 101mg

Variations:

Low-Fat

MAKES 18 SERVINGS, 37 GRAMS PER SERVING

Substitute 16 ounces fat-free cream cheese for Neufchâtel cheese.

• **NUTRITIONAL INFORMATION PER SERVING:**
Calories 85, Carbohydrates 10g, Fiber 0g, Sugar 8g, Protein 4g, Fat 3g, Sodium 137mg

Dairy-Free

MAKES 18 SERVINGS, 37 GRAMS PER SERVING

Substitute 16 ounces nondairy cream cheese for Neufchâtel cheese.

• **NUTRITIONAL INFORMATION PER SERVING:**
Calories 106, Carbohydrates 10g, Fiber 0g, Sugar 8g, Protein 2g, Fat 6g, Sodium 196mg

Essence of Black Cake

MAKES 2 CAKES, 20 SERVINGS EACH, 126 GRAMS PER SERVING

The Essence of Black Cake originated in Guyana over one hundred years ago. This recipe is normally made for special occasions such as Christmas and wedding celebrations. The original recipe required that you soak chopped fruit and nuts in the liquor for a year to give it the ultimate flavor. I have reduced the amount of sugar, eggs, butter, rum, brandy, and amaretto. However, this cake is still not recommended for anyone on a therapeutic diet, especially for obesity, diabetes, high blood pressure, or heart disease.

½ pound seedless cherries
1 pound pitted prunes
1 pound seedless raisins
½ cup chopped walnuts
1½ pounds seedless dates
½ pound citron
1½ cups brandy
1½ cups dark rum
⅔ cup amaretto
1½ cups port wine, divided
3 cups soy flour or all-purpose
   unbleached white flour
2 teaspoons baking powder
1½ cups soy margarine
2 cups natural sugar
10 organic eggs, beaten
1 teaspoon vanilla extract
⅛ teaspoon ground allspice
⅛ teaspoon ground nutmeg
3 tablespoons burnt sugar

Drain and rinse cherries and set aside. Place all other fruit and nuts in food processor. Pulse until chopped, then place mixture in a large plastic container. Pour brandy, rum, amaretto, and 1 cup of port wine over processed mixture. Seal container tightly and let stand at room temperature for 12 to 24 hours.

When ready to prepare cake, grease and flour two 10-inch Bundt pans; set aside. Sift together soy flour and baking powder; set aside. Using an electric mixer on medium speed, cream soy margarine and sugar. Add beaten eggs, vanilla extract, allspice, and nutmeg. Gradually blend in flour mixture. Stir in burnt sugar. Use a wooden spoon to stir in fruit and nut mixture until well-blended.

Pour batter into Bundt pans. Bake at 350 degrees for 60 to 75 minutes or until cake begins to pull away from the sides of the pan. Use remaining ½ cup of wine to pour on top of cakes as soon as they come out of the oven. Place pans on a wire rack to cool.

● NUTRITIONAL INFORMATION PER SERVING:
Calories 369, Carbohydrates 61g, Fiber 3.5g, Sugar 40g,
Protein 6g, Fat 6g, Sodium 85mg

Strawberry Shortcake

3 cups whole strawberries, fresh or frozen

¼ cup natural sugar

2 cups all-purpose unbleached white flour

2 teaspoons baking powder

¼ teaspoon salt (optional)

½ cup solid vegetable shortening

2 organic eggs

⅓ cup natural sugar

½ cup soy milk

1 teaspoon vanilla extract

7 ounces nondairy whipped cream substitute

Preheat oven to 450 degrees. Grease and flour two 9-inch cake pans; set aside. Combine whole strawberries and ¼ cup of sugar in a saucepan. Cook for 10 minutes over low heat; set aside.

Sift together flour, baking soda, and salt, if desired. Cut in shortening using 2 dull knives or pastry blender to achieve a mixture that resembles coarse cornmeal. Add eggs, sugar, soy milk, and vanilla extract to flour mixture. Stir batter with a fork to form a sticky, wet dough. Use a spoon to spread dough evenly between two cake pans. Bake for 12 minutes or until a wooden toothpick inserted in center of each layer comes out clean. Place pans on a wire rack to cool.

When cake layers are completely cool, cut each layer in half horizontally. Prepare shortcakes by layering an even amount of strawberries and nondairy topping on each layer.

● **NUTRITIONAL INFORMATION PER SERVING:**
Calories 197, Carbohydrates 27g, Fiber 1g, Sugar 11g, Protein 4g, Fat 9g, Sodium 83mg

● **DIABETIC EXCHANGES:** 1 Starch, 1 Fruit, 1½ Fat

Southern-Style Apple Pie

Sweet Potato Pie

School House Oatmeal Raisin Cookies

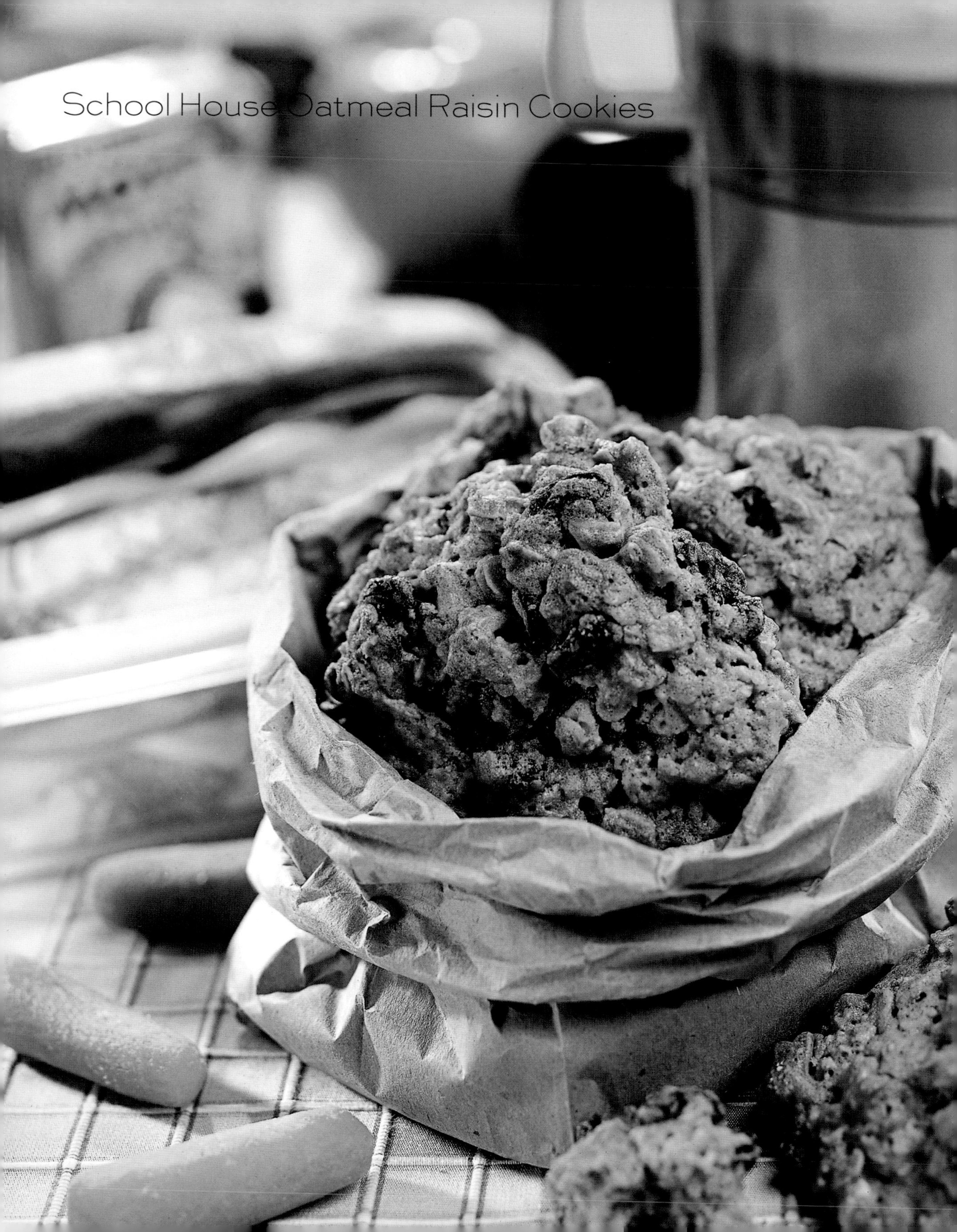

Yellow Cake

MAKES 14 SERVINGS, 80 GRAMS PER SERVING

This is a great basic yellow cake recipe that goes well with Heavenly Chocolate Frosting (page 30) and Chocolate Supreme Cream Cheese Frosting (page 31). This dessert will make any Sunday dinner complete.

2¼ cups all-purpose unbleached white flour
2 teaspoons baking powder
¾ teaspoon salt, optional
¾ cup vegetable shortening
1 cup natural sugar
4 organic eggs
1 cup soy milk
2 teaspoons vanilla extract
1 teaspoon almond extract

Preheat oven to 350 degrees. Grease and flour two 9-inch cake pans; set aside. Sift flour, baking powder, and salt, if desired; set aside.

Cream shortening and sugar; beat well. Add eggs, one at a time, beating after each addition. Gradually mix in flour mixture alternately with soy milk. Stir in vanilla extract and almond extract.

Pour batter into pans. Bake for 25 to 30 minutes or until a wooden toothpick inserted in the center of each layer comes out clean. Place pans on a wire rack to cool.

• NUTRITIONAL INFORMATION PER SERVING:
Calories 257, Carbohydrates 31g, Fiber .23g, Sugar 14g,
Protein 5g, Fat 12g, Sodium 77mg

White Cake

2¼ cups unbleached self-rising white flour
¾ teaspoon salt
¾ cup vegetable shortening
1 cup natural sugar
6 organic egg whites
1 cup soy milk
2 teaspoons clear vanilla extract

This is a great basic white cake recipe that goes well with the delightful blueberry or peach frutti topping found in the cheesecake section on page 70. This is a perfect dessert for picnics and summer cookouts.

Preheat oven to 350 degrees. Grease and flour two 9-inch cake pans; set aside. Sift flour alone first, then add salt and sift again; set aside.

Using an electric mixer on medium speed, cream vegetable shortening and sugar. Add egg whites, one at a time, beating well after each addition. Add flour mixture alternately with soy milk; mix well. Stir in vanilla extract.

Spoon batter into pans. Bake for 25 to 30 minutes or until a wooden toothpick inserted in the center of each layer comes out clean. Place pans on a wire rack to cool.

• NUTRITIONAL INFORMATION PER SERVING:
Calories 235, Carbohydrates 30g, Fiber 1.0g, Sugar 14g, Protein 4, Fat 11g, Sodium 405mg

Cake of Many Flavors

MAKES 14 SERVINGS, 84 GRAMS PER SERVING

A dessert recipe that not only allows you to savor the taste of one cake but several all in one! The variety of flavoring used in this recipe not only gives it a unique taste but is very enjoyable. Try it with the strawberry frutti topping found in the cheesecake section on page 70.

2¼ cups all-purpose
   unbleached white flour
2 teaspoons baking powder
1 teaspoon baking soda
¾ teaspoon salt, optional
¾ cup vegetable shortening
   or soy margarine
1¼ cups natural sugar
4 eggs
1 teaspoon vanilla extract
1 teaspoon almond extract
1 teaspoon coconut extract
1 teaspoon butter flavoring
1 cup soy milk

Preheat oven to 350 degrees. Grease and flour two 9-inch cake pans; set aside. Sift together flour, baking powder, baking soda, and salt, if desired; set aside.

Using an electric mixer on medium speed, cream shortening and sugar. Add eggs, one at a time, beating after each addition. Add vanilla extract, almond extract, coconut extract, and butter flavoring. Add flour mixture, alternating with soy milk, and ending with flour.

Pour batter into pans. Bake 25 to 30 minutes or until a wooden toothpick inserted in the center of each layer comes out clean. Place pans on a wire rack to cool.

• NUTRITIONAL INFORMATION PER SERVING:
Calories 272, Carbohydrates 35g, Fiber .23g, Sugar 17.5g,
Protein 5g, Fat 12g, Sodium 167mg

CHEESECAKES

New York Cheesecake on My Mind: A Tribute to September 11, 2001

I first learned about cheesecake when I was in high school during the 1970s—a time when I learned many things about my body and healthy eating. I went to a dermatologist who told me that if I wanted my acne to disappear I needed to stop eating chocolate and potato chips and to cut back on sugar. I did, lost twenty pounds, and everyone wanted to know how I had done it. But in my then fourteen-year-old opinion, this was too high a price to pay for clear skin. The idea of food, weight, and health being interrelated was new to me, and I grew up in a place where people were not inclined to try something new.

Food was a different story. Cheesecake was definitely new to us, and I was the first one in my family to bake one. I remember it was a package mix by Jell-O. I knew I was a great cook already, but this cheesecake made me want to give up some of my favorite recipes. I must have made cheesecakes for a month straight, and they were all great!

My friends would come over after school so we could talk about our homework, love lives, new outfits, and which teachers got on our nerves most. I would serve cheesecake, and they would say I was going to make a great wife someday because I was such a good cook.

But as I mentioned earlier, a variety of health problems forced me to give up one of my favorite desserts. By the time I got around to developing my Luscious Creamy Cheesecake with a dairy-free alternative, I had not eaten a single slice of cheesecake in over four years! I finally found a way to once again enjoy one of my favorite desserts.

But perhaps the most special cheesecake recipe in this chapter is the very first one. I was working with my cheesecake recipes during the week of September 11, 2001. After watching the horrifying events of that day, I felt very unsettled and stressed, just like the rest of our country. That very same afternoon, I created a special cheesecake I call "New York on My Mind Cheesecake." I first served this cheesecake to the faculty and staff at my school in an effort to help comfort them as they struggled to cope with these tragic events. Although this cheesecake turned out to be delicious, that was almost beside the point; I felt it was my way of giving something back to my community.

All of the cheesecake recipes in this chapter use one of three crusts. I've listed them first, followed by the cheesecake recipes, and ending with several optional toppings you can add to your favorite cheesecake. A number of toppings are made from blueberries, blackberries, or strawberries. If you would like to be daring, you may use fresh peaches and crushed pineapples. Just remember to consider the nutritional values of the toppings if you decide to add them.

All of the cheesecake recipes that follow use one of the following crust recipes. The New York on My Mind Cheesecake and Luscious Creamy Cheesecake are larger, denser cakes that yield 18 servings, so they only use the Springform crust. Allow your crusts to cool completely before adding cheesecake filling.

Natural Graham Springform Crust

MAKES 18 SERVINGS, 16 GRAMS PER SERVING

2 cups crushed whole wheat
  graham crackers
2 tablespoons natural sugar
6 tablespoons soy margarine,
  melted
1 teaspoon ground cinnamon

Combine all ingredients, mixing well. Firmly press crumb mixture evenly over bottom and sides of a 10-inch springform pan. Bake at 325 degrees for 10 minutes.

● **NUTRITIONAL INFORMATION PER SERVING:**
Calories 76, Carbohydrates 11g, Fiber .75g, Sugar 3.5g, Protein 2g, Fat 3g, Sodium 79mg
● **DIABETIC EXCHANGE:** 1 Carbohydrate

Whole Wheat Graham Cracker Crust

MAKES 14 SERVINGS, 16 GRAMS PER SERVING

Combine all ingredients until well mixed. Firmly press mixture evenly over bottom and sides of a 9-inch pie plate. Bake at 325 degrees for 10 minutes.

1½ cups crushed whole wheat graham crackers

1 tablespoon natural sugar

⅓ cup soy margarine, melted

● **NUTRITIONAL INFORMATION PER SERVING:**
Calories 77, Carbohydrates 10g, Fiber .73g, Sugar 3g, Protein 2g, Fat 3g, Sodium 80mg

● **DIABETIC EXCHANGE:** 1 Carbohydrate

Natural Organic Vanilla Wafer Pie Crust

MAKES 14 SERVINGS, 16 GRAMS PER SERVING

Combine all ingredients until well mixed. Firmly press mixture evenly over bottom and sides of a 10-inch springform pan. Bake at 325 degrees for 10 minutes.

1½ cups crushed organic vanilla wafers

1 tablespoon natural sugar

⅓ cup soy margarine or organic unsalted butter, melted

● **NUTRITIONAL INFORMATION PER SERVING:**
Calories 77, Carbohydrates 9g, Fiber .64g, Sugar 5g, Protein 2g, Fat 4g, Sodium 52mg

● **DIABETIC EXCHANGE:** 1 Carbohydrate

New York on My Mind Cheesecake

MAKES 18 SERVINGS, 93 GRAMS PER SERVING

1 Natural Graham Springform
  Crust (page 52)

4 (8-ounce) packages of
  Neufchâtel cheese, softened

¾ cup natural sugar

½ cup soy margarine, melted

2 tablespoons cornstarch

1 teaspoon vanilla extract

2 teaspoons lemon extract

¼ cup soy milk

2 organic eggs

This is a dessert that is traditionally very rich and high in calories. But I created a version using Neufchâtel cheese, fewer eggs, less sugar, and soy milk instead of cream that tastes very similar. This is a dessert to be served with special meals or occasions, such as an anniversary celebration or an afternoon dinner with special friends.

Prepare crust and allow to cool. Preheat oven to 375 degrees. Using an electric mixer on medium speed, beat Neufchâtel cheese, sugar, and melted soy margarine. Add cornstarch, vanilla extract, lemon extract and soy milk; beat well. Add eggs, one at a time, beating after each addition, until smooth and creamy.

Spoon mixture into prepared crust. Bake for 35 to 40 minutes in a 10-inch springform pan. Cool in pan for 40 minutes on wire rack. Cover pan with plastic wrap and freeze for 1 hour, or refrigerate for 3 hours.

● **NUTRITIONAL INFORMATION PER SERVING:**
Calories 296, Carbohydrates 24g, Fiber 1.35g, Sugar 14g, Protein 9g, Fat 18g, Sodium 317mg

Variations:

On the Lighter Side

MAKES 18 SERVINGS, 93 GRAMS PER SERVING

Substitute 32 ounces fat-free cream cheese for the Neufchâtel.

- **NUTRITIONAL INFORMATION PER SERVING:** Calories 213, Carbohydrates 25g, Fiber 1.35g, Sugar 12g, Protein 11g, Fat 7g, Sodium 390mg
- **DIABETIC EXCHANGES:** 2 Lean Meat, 1 Other Carbohydrate

Dairy-Free

MAKES 18 SERVINGS, 93 GRAMS PER SERVING

Substitute 32 ounces nondairy cream cheese for the Neufchâtel.

- **NUTRITIONAL INFORMATION PER SERVING:** Calories 254, Carbohydrates 26g, Fiber 1.35g, Sugar 12g, Protein 8g, Fat 12g, Sodium 507mg

Luscious Creamy Cheesecake

MAKES 18 SERVINGS, 86 GRAMS PER SERVING

1 Natural Graham Springform
   Crust (page 52)
2 envelopes unflavored Emes
   Kosher-Jel or 2 envelopes
   unflavored gelatin
¾ cup natural sugar
¾ cup boiling water
4 (8-ounce) packages
   Neufchâtel cheese, softened
1 teaspoon vanilla extract
2 teaspoons lemon extract

Admittedly, this recipe seems to be somewhat high in fat and calories, but not when compared to a traditional cheesecake recipe. Most traditional cheesecakes use much more sugar and butter, and each serving would normally contain almost double the sugar and fat. For a more intense lemony flavor, add 1 teaspoon of grated lemon zest along with the extracts.

Prepare crust and allow to cool. Mix Emes Kosher-Jel and sugar in a small bowl. Add boiling water. Stir until powder dissolves; set aside.

Using an electric mixer on low speed, beat Neufchâtel cheese until smooth; add vanilla extract and lemon extract. Add dissolved gelatin to cheese, one-third at a time, beating well after each addition. Spoon mixture over prepared crust. Garnish as desired. Refrigerate 2 hours or freeze 30 minutes before serving.

● **NUTRITIONAL INFORMATION PER SERVING:**
Calories 244, Carbohydrates 21g, Fiber .75g, Sugar 13g,
Protein 7g, Fat 15g, Sodium 282mg

Variations:

Lighter Side

MAKES 18 SERVINGS, 86 GRAMS PER SERVING

Substitute 32 ounces fat-free cream cheese for the Neufchâtel.

- **NUTRITIONAL INFORMATION PER SERVING:**
Calories 166, Carbohydrates 23g, Fiber .75g, Sugar 13g, Protein 10g, Fat 3g, Sodium 329mg
- **DIABETIC EXCHANGES:** 1 Low-Fat Milk, ½ Carbohydrate

Dairy-Free

MAKES 18 SERVINGS, 86 GRAMS PER SERVING

Substitute 32 ounces nondairy cream cheese for the Neufchâtel.

- **NUTRITIONAL INFORMATION PER SERVING:**
Calories 202, Carbohydrates 23g, Fiber .75g, Sugar 12g, Protein 6g, Fat 8g, Sodium 472mg
- **DIABETIC EXCHANGES:** ½ Low-Fat Milk, 1 Carbohydrate, 1 Fat

Dreamy Chocolate Cheesecake

MAKES 14 SERVINGS, 73 GRAMS PER SERVING

1 Whole Wheat Graham
   Cracker Crust (page 53)
2 envelopes unflavored Emes
   Kosher-Jel or 2 envelopes
   unflavored gelatin
½ cup natural sugar
¾ cup boiling water
2 (8-ounce) packages
   Neufchâtel cheese, softened
2 teaspoons lemon extract
½ cup of unprocessed Dutch
   cocoa powder or carob
   powder

Prepare crust and allow to cool. Mix Emes Kosher-Jel and sugar in a small bowl. Add boiling water. Stir until powder dissolves; set aside.

Using an electric mixer on low speed, beat Neufchâtel cheese until smooth; add lemon extract. Add gelatin mixture to cheese, one-third at a time, beating well after each addition. Add cocoa powder, beating slowly to blend well. Spoon mixture over prepared crust. Garnish as desired.

Refrigerate for 2 hours or freeze for 30 minutes before serving.

• **NUTRITIONAL INFORMATION PER SERVING:**
Calories 206, Carbohydrates 20g, Fiber 2g, Sugar 11g, Protein 7g, Fat 11g, Sodium 212mg

Variations:

On the Lighter Side

MAKES 14 SERVINGS, 73 GRAMS PER SERVING

Substitute 16 ounces fat-free cream cheese for the Neufchâtel.

• **NUTRITIONAL INFORMATION PER SERVING:**
Calories 153, Carbohydrates 21g, Fiber 2g, Sugar 10g, Protein 8g, Fat 4g, Sodium 259mg
• **DIABETIC EXCHANGES:** 1 Lean Meat, 1 Other Carbohydrate

Dairy-Free

MAKES 14 SERVINGS, 73 GRAMS PER SERVING

Substitute 16 ounces nondairy cream cheese for the Neufchâtel.

• **NUTRITIONAL INFORMATION PER SERVING:**
Calories 179, Carbohydrates 21g, Fiber 2g, Sugar 10g, Protein 6g, Fat 7g, Sodium 334mg
• **DIABETIC EXCHANGES:** 1 Fat, 1 Carbohydrate

Lacey Cinnamon Cheesecake

MAKES 14 SERVINGS, 70 GRAMS PER SERVING

Prepare crust and allow to cool. Mix Emes Kosher-Jel and sugar in a small bowl. Add boiling water. Stir until powder dissolves; set aside.

Using an electric mixer on low speed, beat Neufchâtel cheese until smooth; add vanilla extract, cinnamon, and nutmeg. Add dissolved gelatin to cheese, one-third at a time, beating well after each addition. Spoon mixture over prepared crust. Garnish with carob or chocolate, if desired.

Refrigerate for 2 hours or freeze for 30 minutes before serving.

- **NUTRITIONAL INFORMATION PER SERVING:**
Calories 195, Carbohydrates 19g, Fiber 1g, Sugar 11g, Protein 6g, Fat 11g, Sodium 212mg

1 Whole Wheat Graham
   Cracker Crust (page 53)
2 envelopes unflavored Emes
   Kosher-Jel or 2 envelopes
   unflavored gelatin
½ cup natural sugar
¾ cup boiling water
2 (8-ounce) packages
   Neufchâtel cheese, softened
1 teaspoon vanilla extract
2 teaspoons ground cinnamon
1 teaspoon ground nutmeg
1 ounce melted carob or
   melted semi-sweet
   chocolate, optional, for
   garnish

Variations:

On the Lighter Side

MAKES 14 SERVINGS, 70 GRAMS PER SERVING

Substitute 16 ounces fat-free cream cheese for the Neufchâtel.

- **NUTRITIONAL INFORMATION PER SERVING:**
Calories 142, Carbohydrates 19g, Fiber 1g, Sugar 10g, Protein 7g, Fat 4g, Sodium 259mg
- **DIABETIC EXCHANGES:** 1 Lean Meat, 1 Other Carbohydrate

Dairy-Free

MAKES 14 SERVINGS, 70 GRAMS PER SERVING

Substitute 16 ounces nondairy cream cheese for the Neufchâtel cheese.

- **NUTRITIONAL INFORMATION PER SERVING:**
Calories 168, Carbohydrates 20g, Fiber 1g, Sugar 10g, Protein 5g, Fat 7g, Sodium 334mg
- **DIABETIC EXCHANGES:** 1 Fat, 1 Carbohydrate

Sweeter Than Sweet Potato Cheesecake

MAKES 14 SERVINGS, 86 GRAMS PER SERVING

1 Whole Wheat Graham
   Cracker Crust (page 53)
1 large sweet potato, baked
   and peeled
1 teaspoon ground cinnamon
½ teaspoon ground nutmeg
1½ envelopes unflavored Emes
   Kosher-Jel or 1½ envelopes
   unflavored gelatin
¾ cup natural sugar
¾ cup boiling water
2 (8-ounce) packages
   Neufchâtel cheese, softened
2 teaspoons vanilla extract

Prepare crust and allow to cool. Mash baked sweet potato with cinnamon and nutmeg; set aside. Mix Emes Kosher-Jel and sugar in a small bowl. Add boiling water. Stir until powder dissolves; set aside.

Using an electric mixer on low speed, beat Neufchâtel cheese until smooth; add vanilla extract. Add dissolved mixture to cheese, one-third at a time, beating well after each addition. In a separate bowl, combine one-third of the cheese mixture with the seasoned mashed sweet potato; reserve.

Spoon the plain cheese mixture into a prepared crust. Chill in the freezer for 10 minutes. Remove, and spoon reserved sweet potato and cheese mixture over chilled mixture. Chill in refrigerator before slicing and serving.

● **NUTRITIONAL INFORMATION PER SERVING:**
Calories 221, Carbohydrates 25g, Fiber 1g, Sugar 16g, Protein 6g, Fat 11g, Sodium 213mg

Variations:

On the Lighter Side

MAKES 14 SERVINGS, 86 GRAMS PER SERVING

Substitute 16 ounces fat-free cream cheese for the Neufchâtel cheese.

- **NUTRITIONAL INFORMATION PER SERVING:** Calories 168, Carbohydrates 26g, Fiber 1g, Sugar 15g, Protein 7g, Fat 4g, Sodium 260mg
- **DIABETIC EXCHANGES:** 1 Lean Meat, 1 Other Carbohydrate, 1 Vegetable

Dairy-Free

MAKES 14 SERVINGS, 86 GRAMS PER SERVING

Substitute 16 ounces nondairy cream cheese for the Neufchâtel cheese.

- **NUTRITIONAL INFORMATION PER SERVING:** Calories 194, Carbohydrates 26g, Fiber 1g, Sugar 15g, Protein 5, Fat 7g, Sodium 335mg
- **DIABETIC EXCHANGES:** 1 Fat, 1 Carbohydrate, 1 Vegetable

Perfect Pineapple Cheesecake

MAKES 14 SERVINGS, 87 GRAMS PER SERVING

This is a fabulous cheesecake that reminds me of the old Jell-O cheesecake, only healthier.

Prepare crust and allow to cool. Mix Emes Kosher-Jel and sugar in a small bowl. Add boiling water. Stir until powder dissolves; set aside.

Using an electric mixer on low speed, beat Neufchâtel cheese until smooth; add pineapple extract. Add dissolved gelatin to cheese, one-third at a time, beating after each addition. Arrange pineapple slices on bottom of prepared crust. Reserve 2 slices for garnish. Sprinkle with 1 tablespoon of sugar. Spoon cheese mixture over pineapple slices.

Cut remaining pineapple slices into 4 pieces and place on top and in the center of the cheesecakes. Refrigerate for 2 hours or freeze for 30 minutes before serving.

1 Whole Wheat Graham
 Cracker Crust (page 53)
2 envelopes unflavored Emes
 Kosher-Jel or 2 envelopes
 unflavored gelatin
½ cup natural sugar
¾ cup boiling water
2 (8-ounce) packages
 Neufchâtel cheese, softened
2 teaspoons pineapple extract
1 (8-ounce) can unsweetened
 pineapple slices, drained
1 tablespoon natural sugar

● **NUTRITIONAL INFORMATION PER SERVING:**
Calories 206, Carbohydrates 21g, Fiber .87g, Sugar 14g,
Protein 6g, Fat 11g, Sodium 213mg

Variations:

Low-Fat

MAKES 14 SERVINGS, 87 GRAMS PER SERVING

Substitute 16 ounces fat-free cream cheese for the Neufchâtel cheese.

- **NUTRITIONAL INFORMATION PER SERVING:**
Calories 153, Carbohydrates 22g, Fiber .87g, Sugar 13g, Protein 7g, Fat 4g, Sodium 260mg
- **DIABETIC EXCHANGES:** 1 Lean Meat, 1 Other Carbohydrate

Dairy-Free

MAKES 14 SERVINGS, 87 GRAMS PER SERVING

Substitute 16 ounces nondairy cream cheese for the Neufchâtel cheese.

- **NUTRITIONAL INFORMATION PER SERVING:**
Calories 179, Carbohydrates 23g, Fiber .87g, Sugar 13g, Protein 5g, Fat 7g, Sodium 335mg
- **DIABETIC EXCHANGES:** 1 Fat, 1 Carbohydrate

Luscious Cherry Cheesecake

MAKES 14 SERVINGS, 75 GRAMS PER SERVING

1 Whole Wheat Graham
    Cracker Crust (page 53)
2 envelopes unflavored Emes
    Kosher-Jel or 2 envelopes
    unflavored gelatin
½ cup natural sugar
¾ cup boiling water
2 (8-ounce) packages
    Neufchâtel cheese, softened
2 teaspoons vanilla extract
½ cup fresh, finely chopped
    cherries
Pitted cherries optional, for
    garnish

Prepare crust and allow to cool. Mix Emes Kosher-Jel and sugar in a small bowl. Add boiling water and stir until powder dissolves; set aside.

Using an electric mixer on low speed, beat cheese until smooth; add vanilla extract. Add dissolved gelatin to cheese, one-third at a time, beating well after each addition. Stir in chopped cherries with a wooden spoon or rubber spatula.

Spoon mixture into prepared crust. Garnish with whole cherries, if desired. Refrigerate for 2 hours or freeze for 30 minutes before serving.

● **NUTRITIONAL INFORMATION PER SERVING:**
Calories 198, Carbohydrates 19g, Fiber 1g, Sugar 12g, Protein 6g, Fat 11g, Sodium 212mg

Variations:

On the Lighter Side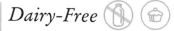

MAKES 14 SERVINGS, 75 GRAMS PER SERVING

Substitute 16 ounces fat-free cream cheese for the Neufchâtel cheese.

● **NUTRITIONAL INFORMATION PER SERVING:**
Calories 145, Carbohydrates 20g, Fiber .85g, Sugar 11g, Protein 7g, Fat 4g, Sodium 259mg
● **DIABETIC EXCHANGES:** 1 Lean Meat, 1 Other Carbohydrate

Dairy-Free

MAKES 14 SERVINGS, 75 GRAMS PER SERVING

Substitute 16 ounces nondairy cream cheese for the Neufchâtel cheese.

● **NUTRITIONAL INFORMATION PER SERVING:**
Calories 171, Carbohydrates 20g, Fiber .85g, Sugar 11g, Protein 5g, Fat 7g, Sodium 334mg
● **DIABETIC EXCHANGES:** 1 Fat, 1 Carbohydrate

Tutti Frutti Cheesecake

MAKES 14 SERVINGS, 84 GRAMS PER SERVING

Prepare crust and allow to cool. Combine Emes Kosher-Jel (or gelatin) and sugar in a small bowl. Add boiling water. Stir until powder dissolves; set aside.

Using an electric mixer on low speed, beat Neufchâtel cheese until smooth. Add vanilla extract and almond extract to cheese. Add dissolved gelatin to cheese, one-third at a time, beating well after each addition. Add ¼ cup cherries and all of the pineapple to cheese mixture; mix well. Pour into prepared crust. Garnish top with remaining ¼ cup cherries.

Refrigerate for 2 hours or freeze for 30 minutes before serving.

- **NUTRITIONAL INFORMATION PER SERVING:**
Calories 204, Carbohydrates 20g, Fiber .73g, Sugar 13g, Protein 6g, Fat 11g, Sodium 212mg

1 Whole Wheat Graham
    Cracker Crust (page 53)
2 envelopes unflavored Emes
    Kosher-Jel or 2 envelopes
    unflavored gelatin
½ cup natural sugar
¾ cup boiling water
2 (8-ounce) packages
    Neufchâtel cheese, softened
1 teaspoon vanilla extract
2 teaspoons almond extract
½ cup fresh sweet cherries,
    divided
½ cup crushed, drained
    pineapple

Variations:

On the Lighter Side

MAKES 14 SERVINGS, 84 GRAMS PER SERVING

Substitute 16 ounces fat-free cream cheese for the Neufchâtel cheese.

- **NUTRITIONAL INFORMATION PER SERVING:**
Calories 150, Carbohydrates 21g, Fiber .73g, Sugar 12g, Protein 7g, Fat 4g, Sodium 260mg
- **DIABETIC EXCHANGES:** 1 Lean Meat, 1 Other Carbohydrate

Dairy-Free

MAKES 14 SERVINGS, 84 GRAMS PER SERVING

Substitute 16 ounces nondairy cream cheese for the Neufchâtel cheese.

- **NUTRITIONAL INFORMATION PER SERVING:**
Calories 177, Carbohydrates 22g, Fiber .73g, Sugar 12g, Protein 5g, Fat 7g, Sodium 334mg
- **DIABETIC EXCHANGES:** 1 Fat, 1 Carbohydrate

Berry Blueberry Cheesecake

MAKES 14 SERVING, 85 GRAMS PER SERVING

Prepare crust and allow to cool. Mix Emes Kosher-Jel and sugar in a small bowl. Add boiling water. Stir until powder dissolves; set aside.

Using an electric mixer on low speed, beat cheese until smooth; add vanilla extract. Add dissolved gelatin to cheese, one-third at a time, beating well after each addition. Add finely chopped blueberries and mix with a wooden spoon or rubber spatula. Spoon over prepared crust. Garnish with whole blueberries and crushed whole wheat graham crackers.

Refrigerate for 2 hours or freeze for 30 minutes before serving.

NUTRITIONAL INFORMATION PER SERVING:
Calories 202, Carbohydrates 20g, Fiber 1g, Sugar 13g, Protein 6g, Fat 11g, Sodium 212mg

1 Whole Wheat Graham Cracker Crust (page 53)

2 envelopes unflavored Emes Kosher-Jel or 2 envelopes unflavored gelatin

½ cup natural sugar

¾ cup boiling water

2 (8-ounce) packages Neufchâtel cheese, softened

1 teaspoon vanilla extract

½ cup fresh or frozen blueberries, finely chopped and drained

1 cup fresh or frozen blueberries

½ cup crushed whole wheat graham crackers

Variations:

On the Lighter Side

MAKES 14 SERVINGS, 85 GRAMS PER SERVING

Substitute 16 ounces fat-free cream cheese for the Neufchâtel cheese.

- **NUTRITIONAL INFORMATION PER SERVING:**
Calories 149, Carbohydrates 21g, Fiber 1g, Sugar 12g, Protein 8g, Fat 4g, Sodium 260mg
- **DIABETIC EXCHANGES:** 1 Lean Meat, 1 Other Carbohydrate

Dairy-Free

MAKES 14 SERVINGS, 85 GRAMS PER SERVING

Substitute 16 ounces nondairy cream cheese for the Neufchâtel cheese.

- **NUTRITIONAL INFORMATION PER SERVING:**
Calories 175, Carbohydrates 22g, Fiber 1g, Sugar 12g, Protein 5g, Fat 7g, Sodium 335mg
- **DIABETIC EXCHANGES:** 1 Fat, 1 Carbohydrate

Blackberry Cheesecake

MAKES 14 SERVINGS, 93 GRAMS PER SERVING

1 Whole Wheat Graham
  Cracker Crust (page 53)
2 envelopes unflavored Emes
  Kosher-Jel or 2 envelopes
  unflavored gelatin
½ cup natural sugar
¾ cup boiling water
2 (8-ounce) packages
  Neufchâtel cheese, softened
1 teaspoon lemon extract
1 teaspoon vanilla extract
½ cup blackberry jelly
½ cup blackberry jam

Prepare crust and allow to cool. Combine Emes Kosher-Jel and sugar in a small bowl. Add boiling water. Stir until powder dissolves; set aside.

Using an electric mixer on low speed, beat Neufchâtel cheese until smooth; add lemon extract and vanilla extract. Add dissolved gelatin to cheese, one-third at a time, beating well after each addition. Add blackberry jelly and beat well. Stir in blackberry jam slowly with wooden spoon or rubber spatula. Spoon mixture over prepared crust. Garnish as desired.

Refrigerate for 2 hours or freeze for 30 minutes before serving.

● **NUTRITIONAL INFORMATION PER SERVING:**
Calories 251, Carbohydrates 33g, Fiber .73g, Sugar 25g,
Protein 6g, Fat 11g, Sodium 212mg

Variations:

On the Lighter Side

MAKES 14 SERVINGS, 93 GRAMS PER SERVING

Substitute 16 ounces fat-free cream cheese for the Neufchâtel cheese.

● **NUTRITIONAL INFORMATION PER SERVING:**
Calories 198, Carbohydrates 34g, Fiber .73g,
Sugar 24g, Protein 7g, Fat 4g, Sodium 260mg

Dairy-Free

MAKES 14 SERVINGS, 93 GRAMS PER SERVING

Substitute 16 ounces nondairy cream cheese for the Neufchâtel cheese.

● **NUTRITIONAL INFORMATION PER SERVING:**
Calories 224, Carbohydrates 34g, Fiber .73g,
Sugar 24g, Protein 5g, Fat 7g, Sodium 334mg

Banana Pudding Cheesecake

MAKES 14 SERVINGS, 86 GRAMS PER SERVING

Prepare crust and allow to cool. Mash bananas with cinnamon and set aside. Mix Emes Kosher-Jel and sugar in a small bowl. Add boiling water. Stir until powder dissolves; set aside.

Using an electric mixer on low speed, beat cheese until smooth; add lemon extract. Add dissolved gelatin to cheese, one-third at a time, beating well after each addition. Add bananas and blend well. Spoon mixture over prepared crust. Garnish with additional sliced bananas, if desired.

Refrigerate for 2 hours or freeze for 30 minutes before serving.

1 Organic Vanilla Wafer Crust
  (page 53)
2 medium ripe bananas
1 teaspoon ground cinnamon
1½ envelopes unflavored Emes
  Kosher-Jel or 1½ envelopes
  unflavored gelatin
½ cup natural sugar
¾ cup boiling water
2 (8-ounce) packages
  Neufchâtel cheese, softened
2 teaspoons lemon extract

● **NUTRITIONAL INFORMATION PER SERVING:**
Calories 209, Carbohydrates 22g, Fiber 1g, Sugar 16g, Protein 6g,
Fat 11g, Sodium 184mg

Variations:

On the Lighter Side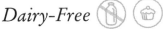

MAKES 14 SERVINGS, 86 GRAMS PER SERVING

Substitute 16 ounces fat-free cream cheese for the Neufchâtel cheese.

● **NUTRITIONAL INFORMATION PER SERVING:**
Calories 156, Carbohydrates 23g, Fiber 1g,
Sugar 15g, Protein 7g, Fat 4g, Sodium 230mg
● **DIABETIC EXCHANGES:** 1 Fat, 1½ Other
Carbohydrate

Dairy-Free

MAKES 14 SERVINGS, 86 GRAMS PER SERVING

Substitute 16 ounces nondairy cream cheese for the Neufchâtel cheese.

● **NUTRITIONAL INFORMATION PER SERVING:**
Calories 182, Carbohydrates 23g, Fiber 1g,
Sugar 15g, Protein 5g, Fat 7g, Sodium 306mg
● **DIABETIC EXCHANGES:** 1 Fat, 1½ Carbohydrate

Frutti Topping for Cheesecake

MAKES 14 SERVINGS, 54 GRAMS PER SERVING

3 cups fresh or frozen
   strawberries
⅓ to ½ cup water
3 tablespoons cornstarch
½ cup natural sugar
2 teaspoons lemon juice

You can use just about any fruit for this recipe—sliced strawberries, peaches, blueberries, blackberries, peaches, mango, pineapple— in just about any combination. This topping is especially good with New York on My Mind Cheesecake or Luscious Creamy Cheesecake.

If using frozen berries, thaw. Mix fruit and remaining ingredients and bring to a boil. Reduce heat and cook until mixture thickens. Remove from heat. Cool before topping cheesecake.

● **NUTRITIONAL INFORMATION PER SERVING:**
Calories 45, Carbohydrates 11g, Fiber .86g, Sugar 9g, Protein .23g, Fat .14g, Sodium 1mg
● **DIABETIC EXCHANGES:** 1 Fruit

Cinnamon Pecan Garnish

MAKES 14 SERVINGS, 4.7 GRAMS PER SERVING

Use this nutty topping with any of the cheesecakes.

Place pecans, cinnamon, and sugar in a saucepan and heat until sugar melts, stirring to coat nuts. Cool and sprinkle over cheesecake.

½ cup crushed pecans

1 teaspoon cinnamon

1 teaspoon natural sugar

NUTRITIONAL INFORMATION PER SERVING:
Calories 31, Sugar 1g, Protein 0g, Fat 3g, Sodium 0mg

PIES AND PUDDINGS

I was raised in rural Yazoo and Holmes counties, Mississippi, and moved several times during my childhood. But regardless of where we lived, there was always a large fruit orchard filled with Red Delicious apples, Granny Smith apples, yellow apples, peaches, pears, plums, muscadines, and blackberries. My mother taught us early how to select fruit for baking, and she would send us out early in the morning to pick fruit for her pies and cobblers. My mother always made the best pies around. Her crusts were so thin and flaky that they seemed to melt in your mouth. People came from all over to taste my mom's sweet potato pie. Some people had a favorite pie, but for us, *every* pie was a favorite.

As I began to modify my mom's pie recipes, I became overwhelmed by the memories that each one evoked. I hope that my pie recipes reflect my mother's years of labor. After tasting my pies she was excited and said, "Baby, these are better than the ones I make, and they are lighter, too."

When ingredients to make other desserts were scarce, my mother would use leftovers such as rice and old bread to make delicious bread or rice puddings. The only exception to this was the banana pudding. For this recipe, she used only fresh bananas and other ingredients such as whole milk, eggs, white sugar, vanilla and lemon flavors, and, of course, vanilla wafers! My version uses fresh bananas, but I substitute soy milk, natural sugar, natural wafer cookies, and organic eggs. The recipe is so light that you can eat it for breakfast, which is why I call it "Morning Pudding."

The bread pudding recipe has also been modified by using wheat or oat bread, soy margarine, and natural sugar.

The following recipes also use high-quality fruit, soy margarine, soy butter, and soy milk instead of the traditional dairy-based products. And by using natural sugar, I was able to reduce the amount of sugar in many recipes by as much as one-half that of white sugar.

Naturally Yours and More (NYM) Pie Pastry

½ cup unbleached white flour

½ cup whole wheat flour

¼ teaspoon salt

3 tablespoons vegetable shortening, chilled

4 tablespoons water

MAKES ONE 9" PIE CRUST (10 SERVINGS, 23 GRAMS PER SERVING)

Place flours and salt in a bowl. Cut shortening into the flour mixture until it resembles coarse crumbs. Drizzle a small amount of water over a portion of the flour mixture and use a fork to blend with flour. Add remaining water and form pastry into a ball. Do not overwork. Wrap in wax paper or plastic wrap and chill for approximately 30 minutes.

Place pastry on lightly floured surface and knead until smooth. Roll out to fit 9-inch pie pan.

● **NUTRITIONAL INFORMATION PER SERVING:**

Calories 81, Carbohydrates 10g, Fiber 1g, Sugar 0g, Protein 2g, Fat 4g, Sodium .58mg

GREAT PASTRY TIPS

1 | Use ice or chilled water to maintain a firmer dough; this makes it less sticky and easier to handle.

2 | After you have formed dough into a ball, wrap it in wax paper, foil, or plastic wrap and chill. Your dough will be easier to roll and shape. Because less flour is needed, your pastry will be more tender.

3 | Roll and shape dough with quick, light strokes on a lightly floured surface.

4 | Try using a broad spatula to occasionally lift pastry so that you can lightly flour the bottom surface. Lift pastry and place in pie pan.

5 | Use a double batch of pie pastry if you want a top and bottom crust. This will be more than enough pastry for you to make a decorative edge or use the left-over pastry to cut out with cookie cutters, lightly bake, and brush with fruit toppings or jam to make an extra treat.

Southern-Style Apple Pie

2 batches NYM Pie Pastry
(page 74)

5 cups Granny Smith apples,
peeled and sliced

¾ cup natural sugar,
1 teaspoon reserved

3 tablespoons unbleached flour

1 teaspoon ground cinnamon

1 teaspoon nutmeg

2 teaspoons soy margarine or
organic unsalted butter, cut
into 4 pieces

Prepare pie pastry. Preheat oven to 375 degrees. Rub a 1 teaspoon of oil or soy margarine in 9-inch pie pan, and line pan with 1 batch of pastry; set aside.

In a large bowl, combine apples, natural sugar, flour, cinnamon, and nutmeg, stirring to completely coat apple slices. Let mixture stand for 10 minutes.

Spoon mixture into pie pastry, spreading evenly. Top pie with second batch of pastry; trim the edges and cut 3 slits in the pastry to allow steam to escape. Dust with reserved 1 teaspoon natural sugar and soy margarine.

Bake at 375 degrees for 50 minutes. Cool on wire rack.

● **NUTRITIONAL INFORMATION PER SERVING:**

Calories 269, Carbohydrates 46g, Fiber 3g, Sugar 22g, Protein 4g, Fat 8g, Sodium 121mg

Variation:

MAKES 10 SERVINGS, 97 GRAMS PER SERVING

This pie also works well with the one-crust pastry. Simply use only the bottom pastry and dot filling with reserved sugar and soy margarine.

● **NUTRITIONAL INFORMATION PER SERVING:**

Calories 186, Carbohydrates 35g, Fiber 2g, Sugar 21.5g, Protein 2g, Fat 4g, Sodium 63mg

Blackberry Pie

MAKES 10 SERVINGS, 98 GRAMS PER SERVING

Prepare pie pastry. Preheat oven to 375 degrees. Mix black-berries and sugar in a large bowl with a wooden spoon or rubber spatula and let stand for 15 minutes. Gently fold flour into blackberries.

Spoon berries into a 9-inch pie pan. Top berries with pie pastry, cut three slits in top to allow steam to escape, and top with soy margarine pieces. Dust pie with reserved teaspoon of sugar.

Bake for 50 minutes. Cool on wire rack.

1 batch NYM Pie Pastry (page 74)

4 cups fresh or frozen blackberries

¾ cup natural sugar, 1 teaspoon reserved

2 tablespoons unbleached white flour

2 teaspoons soy margarine, broken into small pieces

● **NUTRITIONAL INFORMATION PER SERVING:**
Calories 182, Carbohydrates 34g, Fiber 4g, Sugar 19g, Protein 3g, Fat 4g, Sodium 63mg

Variation:

MAKES 10 SERVINGS, 120 GRAMS PER SERVING

This pie also works well with two one-crust pastries. Sim-ply line pie pan with one batch of pastry, top with the other pastry, trim the edges, and cut three slits in the pastry to allow steam to escape.

● **NUTRITIONAL INFORMATION PER SERVING:**
Calories 263, Carbohydrates 44, Fiber 5g, Sugar 19g, Protein 4g, Fat 8g, Sodium 121mg

Peach Pie

1 batch NYM Pie Pastry
   (page 74)

3½ cups fresh peaches peeled,
   pitted, and sliced, or 3½
   cups frozen peaches, sliced

¾ cup sugar, 1 teaspoon
   reserved

2 tablespoons all-purpose
   unbleached white flour

1 teaspoon ground cinnamon

1 teaspoon ground nutmeg

1 teaspoon vanilla extract

Prepare pastry. Preheat oven to 375 degrees. Mix peaches and sugar and let stand for 10 minutes. Stir in flour, cinnamon, and nutmeg.

In a medium saucepan, cook mixture over low heat for 10 minutes, stirring often. Add vanilla extract and stir to blend.

Pour filling into 9-inch pie pan. Cover mixture with pie pastry. Cut three slits into top to allow steam to escape. Bake for 50 minutes. Cool on wire rack.

● **NUTRITIONAL INFORMATION PER SERVING:**
Calories 174, Carbohydrates 33g, Fiber 2g, Sugar 20g, Protein 2g, Fat 4g, Sodium 59mg

● **DIABETIC EXCHANGES:** 1 Fruit, 1 Starch, 1 Fat

Sweet Potato Pie

MAKES 10 SERVINGS, 97 GRAMS PER SERVING

My mother often served this delicious pie for special occasions. The original recipe was made from sweet potatoes that were boiled until they were soft enough to be mashed. She added plenty of sugar, butter, eggs, milk, vanilla, lemon flavor, and nutmeg. In my sweet potato pie, I have changed the preparation by using just one large or two medium sweet potatoes that are baked instead of boiled. This heightens the flavor and retains the natural sugar in the potatoes so I can further reduce the additional amount of sugar used. This pie will always be welcome at any holiday dinner table.

1 batch NYM Pie Pastry
    (page 74)
2 medium sweet potatoes,
    baked, peeled, and mashed
⅓ cup natural sugar
½ cup soy margarine, softened
2 organic eggs
1 teaspoon ground cinnamon
1 teaspoon ground nutmeg
2 teaspoons vanilla extract
1 teaspoon lemon extract
¼ teaspoon salt
2 teaspoons cornstarch
½ cup vanilla soy milk

Prepare pastry. Preheat oven to 325 degrees. Rub 1 teaspoon of oil or soy margarine in 9-inch pie pan, and line pan with pastry; set aside.

Combine sweet potato, natural sugar, soy margarine, organic eggs, cinnamon, nutmeg, vanilla extract, lemon extract, and salt in a large mixing bowl. Using an electric mixer on medium speed, beat potato mixture until light and fluffy. Add cornstarch. Gradually blend in soy milk.

Pour mixture into pie pastry and spread evenly with a rubber spatula. Bake for 20 minutes. Increase oven temperature to 375 degrees and bake for an additional 45 to 50 minutes or until set. Cool on wire rack before cutting into slices.

● **NUTRITIONAL INFORMATION PER SERVING:**
Calories 241, Carbohydrates 30g, Fiber 2.5g, Sugar 12g,
Protein 6g, Fat 10g, Sodium 191mg
● **DIABETIC EXCHANGES:** 2 Starch, 2 Fat

Pumpkin Pie

1 batch NYM Pie Pastry
(page 74)
1 (16-ounce) can solid-pack
pumpkin (do not use
pumpkin pie mix)
⅔ cup natural sugar
Egg substitute equal to 3 eggs,
slightly beaten
1 teaspoon ground cinnamon
1 teaspoon ground nutmeg
¼ teaspoon salt
2 teaspoons vanilla extract
2 teaspoons cornstarch
1 cup plus 2 tablespoons vanilla
soy milk

Prepare pastry. Preheat oven to 325 degrees. Rub 1 teaspoon of oil or soy margarine in 9-inch pie pan, and line pan with pastry; set aside.

Combine pumpkin, sugar, egg substitute, cinnamon, nutmeg, and salt in a large bowl. Using an electric mixer on medium speed, beat pumpkin mixture until light and fluffy. Add vanilla extract and cornstarch; blend in soy milk.

Spoon mixture into prepared pie pastry and bake for 20 minutes. Increase oven temperature to 375 degrees and bake for an additional 45 to 50 minutes until set. Cool on wire rack before cutting into slices.

• **NUTRITIONAL INFORMATION PER SERVING:**
Calories 175, Carbohydrates 29g, Fiber 3g, Sugar 16g, Protein 5g, Fat 4g, Sodium 109mg
• **DIABETIC EXCHANGES:** 1½ Starch, 1 Vegetable, ½ Fat

Mighty Dang Good Pie
(The Preacher's Pie)

MAKES 10 SERVINGS, 105 GRAMS PER SERVING

The story goes that this pie was made for a church picnic. As always, the preacher gets the first slice of every dessert. On the first bite, a large grin came across his face, and he mumbled, "This is a . . . pie." His mouth was so full of pie, that no one could quite hear what he said at first, until he finally blurted out, "This is a Mighty Dang Good Pie!" I have modified this recipe using natural sugar, egg substitute, unsweetened coconut, and unsweetened crushed pineapple. The combination of these ingredients poured and baked in a whole grain pastry shell make an extra special dessert for any occasion.

1 batch NYM Pie Pastry (page 74)

6 tablespoons soy margarine, melted

¾ cup natural sugar

Egg substitute equivalent to 3 eggs

1 cup canned unsweetened pineapple, crushed and drained

1 cup unsweetened coconut flakes

3 tablespoons unbleached white flour

Prepare pie pastry. Preheat oven to 350 degrees. Place pie pastry into a 9-inch pie pan.

Combine ingredients in order with an electric mixer set on medium speed. Pour filling into pie pastry. Bake for 1 hour or until filling is set and golden brown. Cool on wire rack before serving.

● **NUTRITIONAL INFORMATION PER SERVING:**
Calories 283, Carbohydrates 39g, Fiber 2.5g, Sugar 23g, Protein 7g, Fat 12g, Sodium 174mg

Good Ol' Coconut Pie

1 batch NYM Pie Pastry
  (page 74)
½ cup natural sugar
½ cup soy margarine
2 eggs
1 cup soy milk
4 ounces unsweetened coconut
  flakes
1 teaspoon vanilla extract
½ cup all-purpose unbleached
  white flour

Prepare pie pastry. Preheat oven to 325 degrees. Place pie pastry into a 9-inch pie pan.

Using a mixer on medium speed, blend sugar and soy margarine until creamy and fluffy. Add eggs, one at a time, beating well after each addition. Blend in soy milk, coconut, vanilla extract, and flour.

Pour mixture into pie pastry. Bake for 40 minutes or until filling is firm and a toothpick inserted in the center comes out clean. Continue baking for an additional 10 minutes or until filling is ready. Remove from oven. Cool on wire rack before serving.

● **NUTRITIONAL INFORMATION PER SERVING:**
Calories 283, Carbohydrates 32g, Fiber 3g, Sugar 12g, Protein 7g, Fat 14g, Sodium 129mg

Custard Pie

Prepare pie pastry. Preheat oven to 400 degrees. Place pie pastry in a 9-inch pie pan. Prick the pastry several times with a fork. Place a buttered piece of foil facedown onto the pie pastry, and line the unbuttered side with dried beans to weight the foil. Bake for 3 to 5 minutes. When cool enough to handle, remove beans and foil from pie pastry.

Reduce oven temperature to 350 degrees. Combine sugar and nutmeg. Using an electric mixer on low speed, add eggs one at a time, beating well after each addition until well blended. Stir in soy milk and vanilla extract with a wooden spoon or rubber spatula.

Cover edge of pie pastry with foil to prevent burning. Pour filling into pastry and spread evenly. Bake for 50 minutes. Cool on wire rack before serving.

1 batch NYM Pastry
(page 74)
⅓ cup natural sugar
1 teaspoon nutmeg
4 organic eggs
2 cups soy milk
2 teaspoons vanilla extract

● **NUTRITIONAL INFORMATION PER SERVING:**
Calories 157, Carbohydrates 18g, Fiber 1g, Sugar 7g, Protein 6g, Fat 7g, Sodium 90mg
● **DIABETIC EXCHANGES:** 1½ Starch, 1 Fat

Chess Pie

1 batch NYM Pie Pastry
(page 74)

1 cup natural sugar

2 tablespoons unbleached
cornmeal

½ cup soy milk

2 tablespoons lemon juice

1 tablespoon lemon zest

4 organic eggs

¼ cup soy margarine, melted
and cooled

1 teaspoon vanilla extract

Preheat oven to 350 degrees. Place pie pastry in a 9-inch pie pan. Prick the pastry several times with a fork. Place a buttered piece of foil facedown onto the pie pastry, and line the unbuttered side with dried beans to weight the foil. Bake for 3 to 5 minutes. When cool enough to handle, remove beans and foil from pie pastry.

Combine sugar and cornmeal; set aside. Combine soy milk, lemon juice, and lemon zest; set aside. Using an electric mixer on medium speed, beat eggs. Stir in sugar mixture, soy milk mixture, melted margarine, and vanilla extract.

Cover edge of pie pastry with foil to prevent burning. Bake for 50 minutes. Cool on wire rack before slicing and serving.

● **NUTRITIONAL INFORMATION PER SERVING:**
Calories 238, Carbohydrates 34g, Fiber 2g, Sugar 20g, Protein 6g, Fat 8.5g, Sodium 112mg

Double Fudge Pie

MAKES 8 SERVINGS, 51 GRAMS PER SERVING

Preheat oven to 325 degrees. Sift flour with cocoa; set aside. Using a mixer on medium speed, blend sugar and soy margarine until creamy and fluffy. Add eggs one at a time, beating well after each addition. Blend in flour mixture. If using, stir in walnuts with a wooden spoon or spatula.

Pour filling into greased 9-inch pie pan. Bake for 25 minutes. Cool on wire rack.

½ cup flour

2 tablespoons Dutch-processed cocoa powder

½ cup natural sugar

½ cup soy margarine

2 organic eggs, or egg substitute equivalent to 2 eggs

½ cup walnuts, optional

● **NUTRITIONAL INFORMATION PER SERVING (DOES NOT INCLUDE OPTIONAL WALNUTS):**
Calories 195, Carbohydrates 25g, Fiber 2g, Sugar 14g, Protein 6g, Fat 8g, Sodium 82mg

● **DIABETIC EXCHANGES:** 1 Starch, 1 Other Carbohydrate, 1 Fat

Baked Rice Pudding

MAKES 12 SERVINGS, 96 GRAMS PER SERVING

2 eggs, or egg substitute equal
    to 2 eggs

2 cups vanilla soy milk

½ cup natural sugar

2 teaspoons vanilla extract

3 tablespoons organic butter,
    melted

1 teaspoon ground nutmeg

1 teaspoon ground cinnamon

¾ cup raisins

1½ cups cooked brown rice

This rice pudding is a pleasant change from the usual, heavy-tasting rice puddings of old. Although influenced by the old-fashioned rice pudding, I have concocted a recipe true to tradition, but I have changed it to be more suitable for present day circumstances. One of the major changes is that eggs or egg substitute can be used in this recipe. In other words, it is healthy for those who need to restrict fat, cholesterol, and sugar. Fiber has been increased by substituting brown rice for white rice.

Preheat oven to 325 degrees. Grease a 13x9x2-inch baking pan; set aside.

Using an electric mixer on medium speed, combine eggs, soy milk, sugar, and vanilla extract. Blend in melted butter, nutmeg, cinnamon, and raisins. Mix in cooked rice with a rubber spatula.

Spoon batter into prepared baking pan. Bake for 30 minutes or until a knife inserted near the center comes out clean.

• **NUTRITIONAL INFORMATION PER SERVING:**
Calories 153, Carbohydrates 26g, Fiber 1.46g, Sugar 17g,
Protein 4g, Fat 4g, Sodium 52mg

• **DIABETIC EXCHANGES:** 2 Carbohydrate

Morning Banana Pudding

MAKES 14 SERVINGS, 131 GRAMS PER SERVING

The original banana pudding is very rich and made by using whole milk and eggs with lots of sugar to make a thick custard poured over bananas and vanilla wafers. My recipe calls for soy milk, natural sugar, eggs, and natural vanilla wafer–style cookies with a hint of cinnamon. I have changed an old family favorite for a dinner dessert to a dish that can be served for breakfast or dinner. Morning pudding is delicious when chilled or served warmed.

Preheat oven to 350 degrees.

To make the custard: Blend sugar and egg yolks until sugar dissolves. Stir in soy milk and place mixture in a double-boiler or heavy pot. Cook for 12 minutes at low temperature. Mix cornstarch with reserved soy milk, then add to custard and continue stirring for an additional 3 minutes until custard thickens. Stir in vanilla and lemon extracts.

To make the filling: Layer cookies to cover the bottom of a 9x11x2-inch baking pan. Add a layer of banana slices over the cookie layer. Alternate layers of cookies and bananas, ending with a cookie layer on top. Pour custard over layers. Set aside.

To make the meringue: Beat egg whites until whites begin to form stiff peaks. Add sugar and vanilla extract; beat up to 1 additional minute to form thick, glossy meringue.

Spread meringue over banana and cookie layers. Brown in oven for 3 to 5 minutes. Do not overbake.

CUSTARD

½ cup natural sugar

3 egg yolks

3 cups vanilla soy milk,
    3 tablespoons reserved

1 teaspoon cornstarch

3 teaspoons vanilla extract

2 teaspoons lemon extract

FILLING

30 natural vanilla wafer–style
    cookies

5 medium-sized ripe bananas,
    sliced

MERINGUE

3 egg whites

1 teaspoon natural sugar

1 teaspoon vanilla extract

● **NUTRITIONAL INFORMATION PER SERVING:**
Calories 168, Carbohydrates 30g, Fiber 1g, Sugar 23g, Protein 4g,
Fat 4g, Sodium 90mg
● **DIABETIC EXCHANGES:** 2 Starch

Old-Fashioned Bread Pudding

MAKES 14 SERVINGS, 86 GRAMS PER SERVING

3 (6-ounce) slices wheat or oat bread

2 tablespoons apple cider vinegar

2¼ cups vanilla soy milk

3 organic eggs, or 2 organic eggs plus 1 egg substitute, beaten slightly

⅔ cup natural sugar

½ cup raisins

2 tablespoons vanilla extract

3 tablespoons soy margarine, melted

Preheat oven to 325 degrees. Place bread on an ungreased cookie sheet. Bake 5 to 10 minutes or until bread dries and hardens. Cool on wire racks.

Break bread into small chunks and place them in a large bowl. Mix vinegar and soy milk together, then add to bread and soak for 10 minutes. Add eggs, sugar, raisins, and vanilla extract.

Spoon mixture into a 13x9x2-inch baking pan. Drizzle with melted butter. Bake for 40 to 50 minutes or until pudding firms. Cool pan on wire rack.

• **NUTRITIONAL INFORMATION PER SERVING:**
Calories 140, Carbohydrates 23g, Fiber 1.39g, Sugar 15g, Protein 4g, Fat 3g, Sodium 113mg

• **DIABETIC EXCHANGES:** 1½ Starch, 1 Fat

FROZEN DELIGHTS

I do not know where you grew up, but summers in Mississippi were really hot with plenty of cotton fields and no air conditioners. My mother was a share-cropper and always watched Woody Assaf's noonday weather forecast to see what the next day had in store for her and her garden. The weatherman was also an important fixture in my life, not because he reported the weather, but because he did an ice cream commercial. In these commercials, Woody would hold a large glass serving dish filled with luscious ice cream. He would place a heaping spoonful in his mouth and make this "Mmmmm" sound to indicate how good the ice cream tasted. Each day he would eat a different flavor. I could not wait to grow up so that I could be like the weatherman and have a different flavor of ice cream each day.

We did eat our share of ice cream in the summer, especially on the Fourth of July. My uncles would travel from Chicago and buy boxes of ice cream for all of us. But my mother would also make her own ice cream, especially when we had company. She prepared the custard on the stove, and it seemed like she cooked it forever! When it was at the right consistency she poured the custard into a can and placed the can in the ice cream bucket. My sisters and I took turns churning the ice cream, and my mother would check on it until it acquired the desired thickness. When it was ready, we all got a half cup of ice cream and I would pray that our guests would not show up so I could get another serving. Sometimes I was lucky, but most times I was not.

The homemade ice cream we used to make had a high fat and sugar content and was prepared using whole milk, rich cream, eggs, and lots of white sugar. My healthier version uses soy milk, rice milk, skim milk, tofu, and a greatly reduced amount of natural sugars.

Life has changed a lot since I was a child. I no longer churn ice cream. Instead, I use a blender and an electric ice cream maker that produces luscious creamy ice cream in 30 minutes. However, I still want to enjoy ice cream frequently, and now that I've created healthful recipes, I can. And like my secret love, Woody Assaf the weatherman, I can even have a different flavor every day.

All of the nutritional values in this section were calculated with the use of soy milk. Substituting rice or skim milk will only change these values slightly.

Vanilla Creamy Delight

MAKES 10 SERVINGS, 117 GRAMS PER SERVING

Place all ingredients in a blender or food processor. Process until smooth; pour into ice cream maker container. Freeze according to manufacturer's instructions.

2 cups vanilla soy milk, rice milk, or skim milk, chilled

1 (12.3-ounce) package firm tofu, chilled

6 ounces Neufchâtel cheese

¾ cup natural sugar

2 teaspoons vanilla extract

● **NUTRITIONAL INFORMATION PER SERVING:**

Calories 146, Carbohydrates 18g, Fiber 0g, Sugar 17g, Protein 5g, Fat 6g, Sodium 100mg

● **DIABETIC EXCHANGES:** ½ Other Carbohydrate, 1 Skim Milk

Variations:

On the Lighter Side

MAKES 10 SERVINGS, 117 GRAMS PER SERVING

Substitute 6 ounces fat-free cream cheese for the Neufchâtel cheese.

● **NUTRITIONAL INFORMATION PER SERVING:**

Calories 119, Carbohydrates 19g, Fiber 0g, Sugar 16g, Protein 6g, Fat 2g, Sodium 124mg

● **DIABETIC EXCHANGES:** ½ Other Carbohydrate, 1 Skim Milk

Dairy-Free

MAKES 10 SERVINGS, 117 GRAMS PER SERVING

Substitute 6 ounces nondairy cream cheese for the Neufchâtel cheese. Use only soy milk or rice milk.

● **NUTRITIONAL INFORMATION PER SERVING:**

Calories 132, Carbohydrates 19, Fiber 0g, Sugar 16g, Protein 5g, Fat 3g, Sodium 164mg

● **DIABETIC EXCHANGES:** ½ Other Carbohydrate, 1 Skim Milk

Chocolate Chip Creamy Delight

MAKES 10 SERVINGS, 128 GRAMS PER SERVING

2 cups vanilla soy milk, rice
  milk, or skim milk, chilled

6 ounces Neufchâtel cheese

1 (12.3-ounce) package firm
  tofu, chilled

¾ cup natural sugar

2 teaspoons vanilla extract

½ cup crushed natural
  chocolate chips

Place all ingredients in a blender or food processor container except for chocolate chips. Process until smooth; pour into ice cream maker container. Stir in chocolate chips. Freeze according to manufacturer's instructions.

● **NUTRITIONAL INFORMATION PER SERVING:**
Calories 202, Carbohydrates 26g, Fiber .63g, Sugar 23g,
Protein 6g, Fat 9g, Sodium 100mg
● **DIABETIC EXCHANGES:** 2 Carbohydrate, 1 Fat

Variations:

On the Lighter Side

MAKES 10 SERVINGS, 128 GRAMS PER SERVING

Substitute 6 ounces fat-free cream cheese for the Neufchâtel cheese.

● **NUTRITIONAL INFORMATION PER SERVING:**
Calories 175, Carbohydrates 26g, Fiber .63g,
Sugar 23g, Protein 7g, Fat 5g, Sodium 124mg
● **DIABETIC EXCHANGES:** 2 Carbohydrate, ½ Fat

Dairy-Free

MAKES 10 SERVINGS, 128 GRAMS PER SERVING

Substitute 6 ounces nondairy cream cheese for the Neufchâtel cheese. Use only soy milk or rice milk.

● **NUTRITIONAL INFORMATION PER SERVING:**
Calories 188, Carbohydrates 26g, Fiber .63g,
Sugar 23g, Protein 6g, Fat 7g, Sodium 164mg
● **DIABETIC EXCHANGES:** 1 Other Carbohydrate,
1 Low-Fat Milk

Chocolate Lover's Creamy Dream

MAKES 10 SERVINGS, 121 GRAMS PER SERVING

Place all ingredients in a blender or food processor. Process until smooth. Pour into ice cream maker container. Freeze according to manufacturer's instructions.

- **NUTRITIONAL INFORMATION PER SERVING:**
Calories 166, Carbohydrates 20g, Fiber .72g, Sugar 17g, Protein 6g, Fat 7g, Sodium 100mg
- **DIABETIC EXCHANGES:** 1½ Carbohydrate, 1 Fat

2 cups vanilla soy milk, rice milk, or skim milk, chilled
1 (12.3-ounce) package firm tofu, chilled
6 ounces Neufchâtel cheese
1 (1-ounce) square unsweetened chocolate, melted
2 tablespoons unsweetened Dutch-processed cocoa
¾ cup natural sugar
1 teaspoon vanilla extract
1 teaspoon lemon extract

Variations:

On the Lighter Side

MAKES 10 SERVINGS, 121 GRAMS PER SERVING

Substitute 6 ounces fat-free cream cheese for the Neufchâtel cheese.

- **NUTRITIONAL INFORMATION PER SERVING:**
Calories 139, Carbohydrates 20g, Fiber .72g, Sugar 16g, Protein 7g, Fat 4g, Sodium 125mg
- **DIABETIC EXCHANGES:** 1 Carbohydrate, ½ Fat

Dairy-Free

MAKES 10 SERVINGS, 121 GRAMS PER SERVING

Substitute 6 ounces nondairy cream cheese for the Neufchâtel cheese. Use only soy milk or rice milk.

- **NUTRITIONAL INFORMATION PER SERVING:**
Calories 152, Carbohydrates 20g, Fiber .72g, Sugar 16g, Protein 5g, Fat 6g, Sodium 164mg
- **DIABETIC EXCHANGES:** 1½ Carbohydrate, 1 Fat

Mississippi Rocky Road Creamy Delight

MAKES 12 SERVINGS, 116 GRAMS PER SERVING

2 cups vanilla soy milk, rice milk, or skim milk, chilled

6 ounces Neufchâtel cheese

1 (12.3-ounce) package firm tofu, chilled

¾ cup natural sugar

2 teaspoons vanilla extract

½ cup semisweet chocolate bits

½ cup unsweetened coconut

⅓ cup finely chopped peanuts or pecans (optional)

Place first five ingredients in a blender or food processor. Process until smooth; pour into ice cream maker container. Freeze according to manufacturer's instructions. Three to five minutes before freezing is complete, add chocolate, coconut, and peanuts, if using, to the maker container. Complete the freezing process.

• **NUTRITIONAL INFORMATION PER SERVING:**
Calories 231, Carbohydrates 24g, Fiber 2g, Sugar 20g, Protein 6g, Fat 13g, Sodium 87mg

Variations:

On the Lighter Side

MAKES 12 SERVINGS, 110 GRAMS PER SERVING

Substitute 6 ounces fat-free cream cheese for the Neufchâtel cheese.

• **NUTRITIONAL INFORMATION PER SERVING:**
Calories 208, Carbohydrates 24g, Fiber .2g, Sugar 20g, Protein 6g, Fat 10g, Sodium 107mg
• **DIABETIC EXCHANGES:** 1½ Carbohydrate, 2 Fat

Dairy-Free

MAKES 12 SERVINGS, 110 GRAMS PER SERVING

Substitute 6 ounces nondairy cream cheese for the Neufchâtel cheese. Use only soy milk or rice milk.

• **NUTRITIONAL INFORMATION PER SERVING:**
Calories 219, Carbohydrates 24g, Fiber .2g, Sugar 20g, Protein 5g, Fat 12g, Sodium 140mg

Mocha Creamy Delight

MAKES 10 SERVINGS, 121 GRAMS PER SERVING

Place all ingredients in a blender or food processor. Process until smooth; pour into ice cream maker container. Freeze according to manufacturer's instructions.

- **NUTRITIONAL INFORMATION PER SERVING:**
Calories 160, Carbohydrates 20g, Fiber .79g, Sugar 17g, Protein 6g, Fat 7g, Sodium 100mg
- **DIABETIC EXCHANGES:** 1½ Carbohydrate, 1 Fat

2 cups vanilla soy milk, rice milk, or skim milk, chilled

6 ounces Neufchâtel cheese

1 (12.3-ounce) package firm tofu

2 tablespoons coffee alternative (such as Kafree), or decaffeinated coffee

⅓ cup Dutch-processed cocoa or carob powder

¾ cup natural sugar

2 teaspoons vanilla extract

Variations:

Low-Fat

MAKES 10 SERVINGS, 121 GRAMS PER SERVING

Substitute 6 ounces fat-free cream cheese for the Neufchâtel cheese.

- **NUTRITIONAL INFORMATION PER SERVING:**
Calories 131, Carbohydrates 21g, Fiber .79g, Sugar 16g, Protein 7g, Fat 2g, Sodium 125mg
- **DIABETIC EXCHANGES:** 1½ Carbohydrate

Dairy-Free

MAKES 10 SERVINGS, 121 GRAMS PER SERVING

Substitute 6 ounces nondairy cream cheese for the Neufchâtel cheese. Use only soy milk or rice milk.

- **NUTRITIONAL INFORMATION PER SERVING:**
Calories 146, Carbohydrates 21g, Fiber .79g, Sugar 16g, Protein 6g, Fat 4g, Sodium 164mg
- **DIABETIC EXCHANGES:** 1½ Carbohydrate, ½ Fat

Peanut Butter Chocolate Creamy Delight

MAKES 12 SERVINGS, 122 GRAMS PER SERVING

¾ cup natural semisweet chocolate, chopped

½ cup natural creamy peanut butter

2 cups vanilla soy milk, rice milk, or skim milk, chilled

6 ounces Neufchâtel cheese

1 (12.3-ounce) package firm tofu, chilled

¾ cup natural sugar

2 teaspoons vanilla extract

Begin melting chopped chocolate in a saucepan over low heat. Remove from heat before chocolate completely melts and stir to complete melting process. Add peanut butter and mix well. Spread mixture on wax paper and place in freezer for 10 to 15 minutes. Remove wax paper from freezer (make certain chocolate is frozen); break into small chips. Set aside.

Place remaining ingredients in a blender or food processor; process until smooth. Pour into an ice cream maker container.

Freeze according to manufacturer's instructions. Three to 5 minutes before freezing cycle is complete, stir in the chocolate peanut butter chips and finish freezing.

● **NUTRITIONAL INFORMATION PER SERVING:**
Calories 255, Carbohydrates 27g, Fiber 1.45g, Sugar 23g, Protein 8g, Fat 14g, Sodium 133mg

Variations:

On the Lighter Side

MAKES 12 SERVINGS, 122 GRAMS PER SERVING

Substitute 6 ounces fat-free cream cheese for the Neufchâtel cheese.

● **NUTRITIONAL INFORMATION PER SERVING:**
Calories 232, Carbohydrates 27g, Fiber 1.45g, Sugar 22g, Protein 9g, Fat 11g, Sodium 154mg

Dairy-Free

MAKES 12 SERVINGS, 122 GRAMS PER SERVING

Substitute 6 ounces nondairy cream cheese for the Neufchâtel cheese. Use only soy milk or rice milk.

● **NUTRITIONAL INFORMATION PER SERVING:**
Calories 255, Carbohydrates 27g, Fiber 1.45g, Sugar 23g, Protein 8g, Fat 14g, Sodium 133mg

Minty Chunky Chocolate Creamy Delight

MAKES 10 SERVINGS, 129 GRAMS PER SERVING

Begin melting chopped chocolate and peppermint extract in a saucepan or double boiler over low heat. Remove from heat before chocolate completely melts. Stir to complete melting process. Set aside to cool, but don't allow to harden.

Combine remaining ingredients and process until smooth in a blender or food processor. Pour into an ice cream maker container.

Freeze according to manufacturer's instructions. Three to 5 minutes before freezing is complete, add melted chocolate and finish freezing.

½ cup natural semisweet chocolate bars, chopped

1 teaspoon peppermint extract

2 cups vanilla soy milk, rice milk, or skim milk, chilled

1 (12.3-ounce) package firm tofu, chilled

6 ounces Neufchâtel cheese

¾ cup natural sugar

2 tablespoons Dutch-processed cocoa powder

1 teaspoon vanilla extract

- **NUTRITIONAL INFORMATION PER SERVING:**
Calories 206, Carbohydrates 26g, Fiber 1g, Sugar 23g, Protein 6g, Fat 9g, Sodium 100mg
- **DIABETIC EXCHANGES:** 2 Carbohydrate, 1 Fat

Variations:

On the Lighter Side

MAKES 10 SERVINGS, 129 GRAMS PER SERVING

Substitute 6 ounces fat-free cream cheese for the Neufchâtel cheese.

- **NUTRITIONAL INFORMATION PER SERVING:**
Calories 179, Carbohydrates 27g, Fiber 1g, Sugar 23g, Protein 7g, Fat 5g, Sodium 125mg
- **DIABETIC EXCHANGES:** 2 Carbohydrate, ½ Fat

Dairy-Free

MAKES 10 SERVINGS, 129 GRAMS PER SERVING

Substitute 6 ounces nondairy cream cheese for the Neufchâtel cheese. Use only soy milk or rice milk.

- **NUTRITIONAL INFORMATION PER SERVING:**
Calories 192, Carbohydrates 27g, Fiber 1g, Sugar 23, Protein 6g, Fat 7g, Sodium 164mg
- **DIABETIC EXCHANGES:** 2 Carbohydrate, 1 Fat

Pistachio Creamy Delight

MAKES 10 SERVINGS, 124 GRAMS PER SERVING

2 cups vanilla soy milk, rice
    milk, or skim milk, chilled
6 ounces Neufchâtel cheese
1 (12.3-ounce) package
    firm tofu, chilled
¾ cup natural sugar
2 teaspoons almond extract
1 teaspoon green food coloring
½ cup pistachio nuts, chopped

Place all ingredients except nuts in a blender or food processor. Process until smooth; pour into ice cream maker container.

Freeze according to manufacturer's instructions. Three to 5 minutes before freezing is complete, stir in nuts and finish freezing.

- **NUTRITIONAL INFORMATION PER SERVING:**
Calories 182, Carbohydrates 20g, Fiber .69g, Sugar 17g, Protein 7g, Fat 9g, Sodium 100mg
- **DIABETIC EXCHANGES:** 1 Carbohydrate, 1½ Fat

Variations:

On the Lighter Side

MAKES 10 SERVINGS, 124 GRAMS PER SERVING

Substitute 6 ounces fat-free cream cheese for the Neufchâtel cheese.

- **NUTRITIONAL INFORMATION PER SERVING:**
Calories 154, Carbohydrates 21g, Fiber .69g, Sugar 17g, Protein 7g, Fat 5g, Sodium 125mg
- **DIABETIC EXCHANGES:** ½ Carbohydrate, 1 Fat

Dairy-Free

MAKES 10 SERVINGS, 124 GRAMS PER SERVING

Substitute 6 ounces nondairy cream cheese for the Neufchâtel cheese. Use only soy milk or rice milk.

- **NUTRITIONAL INFORMATION PER SERVING:**
Calories 168, Carbohydrates 21g, Fiber .69g, Sugar 17g, Protein 6g, Fat 6g, Sodium 164mg
- **DIABETIC EXCHANGES:** ½ Carbohydrate, 1 Low-Fat Milk

Fantasy Praline Creamy Delight

MAKES 10 SERVINGS, 124 GRAMS PER SERVING

Place all ingredients except pecans in a blender or food processor. Process until smooth; pour into ice cream maker container.

Freeze according to manufacturer's instructions. Three to 5 minutes before freezing is complete, stir in nuts, and finish freezing.

2 cups vanilla soy milk, rice milk, or skim milk, chilled
6 ounces Neufchâtel cheese
1 (12.3-ounce) package firm tofu, chilled
½ cup maple syrup
2 teaspoons vanilla butternut extract
½ cup pecans, crushed

- **NUTRITIONAL INFORMATION PER SERVING:**
Calories 171, Carbohydrates 15g, Fiber .61g, Sugar 13g, Protein 6g, Fat 10g, Sodium 101mg
- **DIABETIC EXCHANGES:** 1 Carbohydrate, 2 Fat

Variations:

On the Lighter Side

MAKES 10 SERVINGS, 124 GRAMS PER SERVING

Substitute 6 ounces fat-free cream cheese for the Neufchâtel cheese.

- **NUTRITIONAL INFORMATION PER SERVING:**
Calories 143, Carbohydrates 16g, Fiber .61g, Sugar 12g, Protein 7g, Fat 6g, Sodium 126mg
- **DIABETIC EXCHANGES:** 1 Carbohydrate, ½ Low-Fat Milk

Dairy-Free

MAKES 10 SERVINGS, 124 GRAMS PER SERVING

Substitute 6 ounces nondairy cream cheese for the Neufchâtel cheese. Use only soy milk or rice milk.

- **NUTRITIONAL INFORMATION PER SERVING:**
Calories 157, Carbohydrates 16g, Fiber .61g, Sugar 12g, Protein 5g, Fat 8g, Sodium 165mg
- **DIABETIC EXCHANGES:** ½ Carbohydrate, 1 Low-Fat Milk

Pecan Spice Creamy Delight

MAKES 10 SERVINGS, 127 GRAMS PER SERVING

½ cup pecans, crushed

2 tablespoons maple syrup

2 cups vanilla soy milk, rice milk, or skim milk, chilled

6 ounces Neufchâtel cheese

1 (12.3-ounce) package firm tofu, chilled

¾ cup natural sugar

1 teaspoon vanilla extract

1 teaspoon vanilla butternut extract

Preheat oven to 350 degrees. Place crushed pecans on baking sheet and bake for 1 to 3 minutes, stirring occasionally, until toasted. Mix toasted pecans with maple syrup. Let nuts come to room temperature, then refrigerate until chilled.

Combine all other ingredients in a blender or food processor. Process until smooth; pour into ice cream maker container.

Freeze according to manufacturer's instructions. Three to 5 minutes before freezing is complete, stir in chilled pecans, and finish freezing.

● **NUTRITIONAL INFORMATION PER SERVING:**
Calories 198, Carbohydrates 22g, Fiber .61g, Sugar 19g, Protein 6g, Fat 10g, Sodium 100mg
● **DIABETIC EXCHANGES:** 1½ Carbohydrate, 2 Fat

Variations:

On the Lighter Side

MAKES 10 SERVINGS, 127 GRAMS PER SERVING

Substitute 6 ounces fat-free cream cheese for the Neufchâtel cheese.

● **NUTRITIONAL INFORMATION PER SERVING:**
Calories 170, Carbohydrates 22g, Fiber .61g, Sugar 19g, Protein 7g, Fat 6g, Sodium 126mg
● **DIABETIC EXCHANGES:** 1½ Carbohydrate, 1 Fat

Dairy-Free

MAKES 10 SERVINGS, 127 GRAMS PER SERVING

Substitute 6 ounces nondairy cream cheese for the Neufchâtel cheese. Use only soy milk or rice milk.

● **NUTRITIONAL INFORMATION PER SERVING:**
Calories 184, Carbohydrates 23g, Fiber .61g, Sugar 19g, Protein 5g, Fat 8g, Sodium 164mg
● **DIABETIC EXCHANGES:** 1½ Carbohydrate, 1½ Fat

Toasty Creamy Black Walnut Delight

MAKES 10 SERVINGS, 123 GRAMS PER SERVING

Preheat oven to 350 degrees. Place crushed walnuts on baking sheet and bake for 3 to 5 minutes. Remove from oven and let cool to room temperature before refrigerating.

Place remaining ingredients in a blender or food processor. Process until smooth; pour mixture into ice cream maker container.

Freeze according to manufacturer's instructions. Three to 5 minutes before freezing is complete, stir in chilled walnuts, and finish freezing. Complete the freezing process.

½ cup black walnuts, crushed

2 cups vanilla soy milk, rice milk, or skim milk, chilled

6 ounces Neufchâtel cheese

1 (12.3-ounce) package firm tofu

¾ cup natural sugar

2 teaspoons vanilla extract

- **NUTRITIONAL INFORMATION PER SERVING:**
Calories 185, Carbohydrates 19g, Fiber .46g, Sugar 17g, Protein 7g, Fat 9g, Sodium 100mg
- **DIABETIC EXCHANGES:** 1 Carbohydrate, 1 Fat, ½ Low-Fat Milk

Variations:

On the Lighter Side

MAKES 10 SERVINGS, 123 GRAMS PER SERVING

Substitute 6 ounces fat-free cream cheese for the Neufchâtel cheese.

- **NUTRITIONAL INFORMATION PER SERVING:**
Calories 157, Carbohydrates 20g, Fiber .46g, Sugar 16g, Protein 8g, Fat 6g, Sodium 125mg
- **DIABETIC EXCHANGES:** ½ Other Carbohydrate, 1 Low-Fat Milk

Dairy-Free

MAKES 10 SERVINGS, 123 GRAMS PER SERVING.

Substitute 6 ounces nondairy cream cheese for the Neufchâtel cheese. Use only soy milk or rice milk.

- **NUTRITIONAL INFORMATION PER SERVING:**
Calories 171, Carbohydrates 20g, Fiber .46g, Sugar 16g, Protein 6g, Fat 7g, Sodium 164mg
- **DIABETIC EXCHANGES:** ½ Carbohydrate, 1 Low-Fat Milk

Better Than Banana Delight

MAKES 12 SERVINGS, 112 GRAMS PER SERVING

2 cups vanilla soy milk, rice milk, or skim milk, chilled

6 ounces Neufchâtel cheese

1 (12.3-ounce) package firm tofu, chilled

¾ cup natural sugar

2 teaspoons banana extract

¼ teaspoon cinnamon

1 large ripe banana, mashed

½ cup crushed natural vanilla wafers

⅓ cup crushed pecans (optional)

Place the first 7 ingredients in a blender or food processor. Process until smooth; pour into ice cream maker container.

Freeze according to manufacturer's instructions. Three to 5 minutes before freezing is complete, add mashed banana, vanilla wafers, and crushed pecans, if using, to the ice cream maker container. Complete the freezing process.

● **NUTRITIONAL INFORMATION PER SERVING:**
Calories 147, Carbohydrates 21g, Fiber .39g, Sugar 17g, Protein 5g, Fat 5g, Sodium 94mg
● **DIABETIC EXCHANGES:** ½ Other Carbohydrate, 1 Low-Fat Milk

Variations:

On the Lighter Side

MAKES 12 SERVINGS, 112 GRAMS PER SERVING

Substitute 6 ounces fat-free cream cheese for the Neufchâtel cheese.

● **NUTRITIONAL INFORMATION PER SERVING:**
Calories 124, Carbohydrates 21g, Fiber .39g, Sugar 17g, Protein 5g, Fat 2g, Sodium 114mg
● **DIABETIC EXCHANGES:** ½ Other Carbohydrate, 1 Skim Milk

Dairy-Free

MAKES 12 SERVINGS, 112 GRAMS PER SERVING

Substitute 6 ounces nondairy cream cheese for the Neufchâtel cheese. Use soy milk or rice milk.

● **NUTRITIONAL INFORMATION PER SERVING:**
Calories 135, Carbohydrates 21g, Fiber .39g, Sugar 17g, Protein 4g, Fat 3g, Sodium 147mg
● **DIABETIC EXCHANGES:** 1½ Carbohydrate, ½ Fat

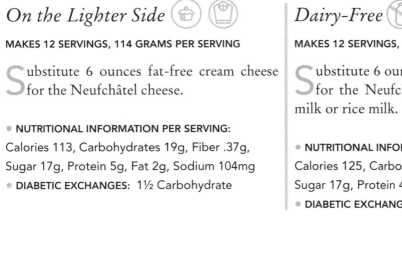

Cherry Dream Creamy Delight

MAKES 12 SERVINGS, 114 GRAMS PER SERVING

Place all ingredients in a blender or food processor. Process until smooth; pour into ice cream maker container. Freeze according to manufacturer's instructions.

- **NUTRITIONAL INFORMATION PER SERVING:**
Calories 136, Carbohydrates 19g, Fiber .37g, Sugar 17g, Protein 5g, Fat 5g, Sodium 83mg
- **DIABETIC EXCHANGES:** 1½ Carbohydrate, ½ Fat

2 cups vanilla soy milk, rice milk, or skim milk, chilled
6 ounces Neufchâtel cheese
1 (12.3-ounce) package firm tofu, chilled
¾ cup natural sugar
2 teaspoons vanilla extract
¾ cup frozen or fresh cherries, pits removed

Variations:

On the Lighter Side

MAKES 12 SERVINGS, 114 GRAMS PER SERVING

Substitute 6 ounces fat-free cream cheese for the Neufchâtel cheese.

- **NUTRITIONAL INFORMATION PER SERVING:**
Calories 113, Carbohydrates 19g, Fiber .37g, Sugar 17g, Protein 5g, Fat 2g, Sodium 104mg
- **DIABETIC EXCHANGES:** 1½ Carbohydrate

Dairy-Free

MAKES 12 SERVINGS, 114 GRAMS PER SERVING

Substitute 6 ounces nondairy cream cheese for the Neufchâtel cheese. Use only soy milk or rice milk.

- **NUTRITIONAL INFORMATION PER SERVING:**
Calories 125, Carbohydrates 20g, Fiber .37g, Sugar 17g, Protein 4g, Fat 3g, Sodium 137mg
- **DIABETIC EXCHANGES:** 1½ Carbohydrate

Tutti Fruitti Creamy Delight

MAKES 12 SERVINGS, 114 GRAMS PER SERVING

6 ounces fresh sweet cherries,
chopped

2 cups vanilla soy milk, rice
milk, or skim milk, chilled

1 (12.3-ounce) package
firm tofu, chilled

6 ounces Neufchâtel cheese

½ cup natural sugar

1 teaspoon vanilla extract

1 teaspoon almond extract

½ cup fresh pineapple,
chopped, or ½ cup canned
unsweetened crushed
pineapple

Rinse cherries and set aside.

Place all ingredients, except cherries and pineapple, in a blender or food processor. Process until smooth. Pour into ice cream maker container.

Freeze according to manufacturer's instructions. During last 10 minutes of freezing, drain cherries and add with pineapple to mixture.

● **NUTRITIONAL INFORMATION PER SERVING:**
Calories 122, Carbohydrates 15g, Fiber .40g, Sugar 13g, Protein 5g, Fat 5g, Sodium 83mg

● **DIABETIC EXCHANGES:** 1 Carbohydrate, 1 Fat

Variations:

On the Lighter Side

MAKES 12 SERVINGS, 114 GRAMS PER SERVING

Substitute 6 ounces fat-free cream cheese for the Neufchâtel cheese.

● **NUTRITIONAL INFORMATION PER SERVING:**
Calories 98, Carbohydrates 16g, Fiber .40g, Sugar 13g, Protein 5g, Fat 2g, Sodium 104mg

● **DIABETIC EXCHANGES:** 1 Carbohydrate, ½ Fat

Dairy-Free

MAKES 12 SERVINGS, 114 GRAMS PER SERVING

Substitute 6 ounces nondairy cream cheese for the Neufchâtel cheese. Use only soy milk or rice milk.

● **NUTRITIONAL INFORMATION PER SERVING:**
Calories 110, Carbohydrates 16g, Fiber .40g, Sugar 13g, Protein 4g, Fat 3g, Sodium 137mg

● **DIABETIC EXCHANGES:** 1 Carbohydrate, ½ Fat

Clown Cone

Prepare the Delight. Place one scoop Creamy Delight in a small chilled dessert dish or bowl and surround the scoop with the fresh fruit. Make a "face" with the reserved fruit and top with the "cone" hat.

1 natural cone

½ cup fresh fruit (chopped apple, blueberries, chopped or crushed pineapple, star fruit, pomegranate, etc.), reserving about 1 tablespoon for decoration

● NUTRITIONAL INFORMATION PER SERVING FOR DECORATION ONLY: Calories 94, Carbohydrate 20g, Fiber 1.74g, Sugar 12g, Protein 1g, Fat 1.27g, Sodium 20mg

● DIABETIC EXCHANGES: 1 Fruit, ½ Carbohydrate

Georgia Peachy Creamy

¾ cup fresh or frozen sliced
   peaches

2 tablespoons water

2 teaspoons natural sugar

2 teaspoons soy margarine,
   divided

¼ teaspoon ground cinnamon

2 cups vanilla soy milk or rice
   milk, chilled

6 ounces Neufchâtel cheese

1 (12.3-ounce) package
   firm tofu

2 tablespoons water

½ cup plus 1 tablespoon
   natural sugar

2 teaspoons vanilla extract

Place peach slices in a saucepan with water, sugar, 1 teaspoon soy margarine, and cinnamon. Bring mixture to a boil. Reduce heat and simmer for 5 minutes. Remove mixture from heat and let cool. Refrigerate for at least 2 hours.

Place all other ingredients in a blender or food processor. Process until smooth; pour mixture into an ice cream maker container.

Freeze according to manufacturer's instructions. Three to 5 minutes before freezing is complete, add chilled peaches to container and finish freezing.

- **NUTRITIONAL INFORMATION PER SERVING:**
Calories 147, Carbohydrates 17g, Fiber .40g, Sugar 15g, Protein 6g, Fat 6g, Sodium 104mg
- **DIABETIC EXCHANGES:** 1 Carbohydrate, ½ Low-Fat Milk

Variations:

On the Lighter Side

MAKES 10 SERVINGS, 134 GRAMS PER SERVING

Substitute 6 ounces fat-free cream cheese for the Neufchâtel cheese.

- **NUTRITIONAL INFORMATION PER SERVING:**
Calories 119, Carbohydrates 18g, Fiber .40g, Sugar 15g, Protein 6g, Fat 2g, Sodium 130mg
- **DIABETIC EXCHANGES:** ½ Low-Fat Milk, 1 Fruit

Dairy-Free

MAKES 10 SERVINGS, 134 GRAMS PER SERVING

Substitute 6 ounces nondairy cream cheese for the Neufchâtel cheese. Use only soy milk or rice milk.

- **NUTRITIONAL INFORMATION PER SERVING:**
Calories 133, Carbohydrates 18g, Fiber .40g, Sugar 15g, Protein 5g, Fat 4g, Sodium 168mg
- **DIABETIC EXCHANGES:** ½ Low-Fat Milk, 1 Fruit

Strawberry Supreme Creamy Delight

MAKES 10 SERVINGS, 124 GRAMS PER SERVING

Place all ingredients in a blender or food processor. Process until smooth; pour into ice cream maker container. Freeze according to manufacturer's instructions.

2 cups vanilla soy milk, rice milk, or skim milk, chilled

6 ounces Neufchâtel cheese

1 (12.3-ounce) package firm tofu, chilled

¾ cup natural sugar

1 teaspoon vanilla extract

1 teaspoon strawberry extract

½ cup fresh or frozen unsweetened strawberries

- **NUTRITIONAL INFORMATION PER SERVING:**
Calories 149, Carbohydrates 19g, Fiber .19g, Sugar 17g, Protein 5g, Fat 6g, Sodium 100mg
- **DIABETIC EXCHANGES:** 1 Low-Fat Milk, ½ Fruit

Variations:

On the Lighter Side

MAKES 10 SERVINGS, 124 GRAMS PER SERVING

Substitute 6 ounces fat-free cream cheese for the Neufchâtel cheese.

- **NUTRITIONAL INFORMATION PER SERVING:**
Calories 121, Carbohydrates 20g, Fiber .19g, Sugar 17g, Protein 6g, Fat 2g, Sodium 125mg
- **DIABETIC EXCHANGES:** 1 Skim Milk, ½ Fruit

Dairy-Free

MAKES 10 SERVINGS, 124 GRAMS PER SERVING

Substitute 6 ounces nondairy cream cheese for the Neufchâtel cheese. Use only soy milk or rice milk.

- **NUTRITIONAL INFORMATION PER SERVING:**
Calories 135, Carbohydrates 20g, Fiber .19g, Sugar 17g, Protein 5g, Fat 3g, Sodium 164mg
- **DIABETIC EXCHANGES:** 1½ Other Carbohydrate, 1 Lean Meat

Triple Treat Sundae

2 cups vanilla soy milk, rice milk, or skim milk, chilled

6 ounces Neufchâtel cheese

1 (12.3-ounce) package firm tofu

¾ cup natural sugar

1 teaspoon vanilla extract

1 teaspoon strawberry extract

½ cup mashed banana

½ cup fresh or frozen strawberries, chopped

2 ounces melted chocolate

Place first six ingredients in a blender or food processor. Process until smooth; pour into ice cream maker container.

Freeze according to manufacturer's instructions. Three to 5 minutes before freezing is complete, add mashed bananas, chopped strawberries, and chocolate. Complete the freezing process.

- **NUTRITIONAL INFORMATION PER SERVING:**
Calories 160, Carbohydrates 19g, Fiber 1g, Sugar 16g, Protein 5g, Fat 7g, Sodium 83mg
- **DIABETIC EXCHANGES:** 1 Carbohydrate, ½ Fruit, 1 Fat

Variations:

On the Lighter Side

MAKES 10 SERVINGS, 124 GRAMS PER SERVING

Substitute 6 ounces fat-free cream cheese for the Neufchâtel cheese.

- **NUTRITIONAL INFORMATION PER SERVING:**
Calories 136, Carbohydrates 20g, Fiber 1g, Sugar 16g, Protein 6g, Fat 4g, Sodium 104mg
- **DIABETIC EXCHANGES:** 1 Carbohydrate, ½ Low-Fat Milk

Dairy-Free

MAKES 10 SERVINGS, 124 GRAMS PER SERVING

Substitute 6 ounces nondairy cream cheese for the Neufchâtel cheese. Use only soy milk or rice milk.

- **NUTRITIONAL INFORMATION PER SERVING:**
Calories 148, Carbohydrates 20g, Fiber 1g, Sugar 16g, Protein 4g, Fat 6g, Sodium 137mg
- **DIABETIC EXCHANGES:** 1 Carbohydrate, ½ Low-Fat Milk

Luscious Lemony Creamy Delight

MAKES 10 SERVINGS, 117 GRAMS PER SERVING

Place all ingredients in a blender or food processor. Process until smooth; pour into ice cream maker container. Freeze according to manufacturer's instructions.

2 cups vanilla soy milk, rice milk, or skim milk, chilled

6 ounces Neufchâtel cheese

1 (12.3-ounce) package firm tofu, chilled

¾ cup natural sugar

2 teaspoons lemon extract

½ teaspoon lemon zest

½ teaspoon natural yellow food coloring

● **NUTRITIONAL INFORMATION PER SERVING:**
Calories 147, Carbohydrates 18g, Fiber 0g, Sugar 17g, Protein 5g, Fat 6g, Sodium 100mg

● **DIABETIC EXCHANGES:** 1 Low-Fat Milk, ½ Carbohydrate

Variations:

On the Lighter Side

MAKES 10 SERVINGS, 117 GRAMS PER SERVING

Substitute 6 ounces fat-free cream cheese for the Neufchâtel cheese.

● **NUTRITIONAL INFORMATION PER SERVING:**
Calories 120, Carbohydrates 19g, Fiber 0g, Sugar 16g, Protein 6g, Fat 2g, Sodium 125mg

● **DIABETIC EXCHANGES:** 1 Skim Milk, ½ Other Carbohydrate

Dairy-Free

MAKES 10 SERVINGS, 117 GRAMS PER SERVING

Substitute 6 ounces nondairy cream cheese for the Neufchâtel cheese. Use only soy milk or rice milk.

● **NUTRITIONAL INFORMATION PER SERVING:**
Calories 132, Carbohydrates 19g, Fiber 0g, Sugar 16g, Protein 5g, Fat 3g, Sodium 164mg

● **DIABETIC EXCHANGES:** 1 Skim Milk, ½ Carbohydrate

Luscious Lime Creamy Delight

MAKES 10 SERVINGS, 117 GRAMS PER SERVING

2 cups vanilla soy milk, rice
    milk, or skim milk, chilled

6 ounces Neufchâtel cheese

1 (12.3-ounce) package
    firm tofu

¾ cup natural sugar

1 teaspoon lemon extract

1 teaspoon lime juice

1 teaspoon lime zest

Place all ingredients in a blender or food processor. Process until smooth; pour into ice cream maker container. Freeze according to manufacturer's instructions.

● **NUTRITIONAL INFORMATION PER SERVING:**
Calories 145, Carbohydrates 18g, Fiber 0g, Sugar 17g, Protein 5g, Fat 6g, Sodium 100mg
● **DIABETIC EXCHANGES:** 1 Low-Fat Milk, ½ Carbohydrate

Variations:

On the Lighter Side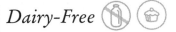

MAKES 10 SERVINGS, 117 GRAMS PER SERVING

Substitute 6 ounces fat-free cream cheese for the Neufchâtel cheese.

● **NUTRITIONAL INFORMATION PER SERVING:**
Calories 117, Carbohydrates 19g, Fiber 0g, Sugar 16g, Protein 6g, Fat 2g, Sodium 124mg
● **DIABETIC EXCHANGES:** 1 Skim Milk, ½ Other Carbohydrate

Dairy-Free

MAKES 10 SERVINGS, 117 GRAMS PER SERVING

Substitute 6 ounces nondairy cream cheese for the Neufchâtel cheese. Use only soy milk or rice milk.

● **NUTRITIONAL INFORMATION PER SERVING:**
Calories 131, Carbohydrates 19g, Fiber 0g, Sugar 16g, Protein 5g, Fat 3g, Sodium 164mg
● **DIABETIC EXCHANGES:** 1 Skim Milk, ½ Carbohydrate

Tutti Fruittie Creamy Delight

Luscious Creamy Cheesecake

Essence of Black Cake

Heavenly Chocolate Cake

Eggnog Creamy Delight

MAKES 10 SERVINGS,125 GRAMS PER SERVING

Place all ingredients in a blender or food processor. Process until smooth; pour into ice cream maker container. Freeze according to manufacturer's instructions.

- **NUTRITIONAL INFORMATION PER SERVING:**
Calories 137, Carbohydrates 14g, Fiber .25g, Sugar 12g, Protein 7g, Fat 6g, Sodium 125mg
- **DIABETIC EXCHANGES:** 1 Carbohydrate, 1 Fat

2 cups vanilla soy milk, chilled
6 ounces Neufchâtel cheese
1 (12.3-ounce) package
    firm tofu, chilled
Egg substitute equal to 2 eggs
½ cup natural sugar
1 teaspoon natural yellow food
    coloring
1 teaspoon ground cinnamon
2 teaspoons ground nutmeg
2 teaspoons vanilla extract

Variations:

On the Lighter Side

MAKES 10 SERVINGS,125 GRAMS PER SERVING

Substitute 6 ounces fat-free cream cheese for the Neufchâtel cheese.

- **NUTRITIONAL INFORMATION PER SERVING:**
Calories 109, Carbohydrates 15g, Fiber .25g, Sugar 12g, Protein 7g, Fat 2g, Sodium 150mg
- **DIABETIC EXCHANGES:** 1 Low-Fat Milk

Dairy-Free

MAKES 10 SERVINGS, 125 GRAMS PER SERVING

Substitute 6 ounces nondairy cream cheese for the Neufchâtel cheese. Use only soy milk or rice milk.

- **NUTRITIONAL INFORMATION PER SERVING:**
Calories 122, Carbohydrates 15g, Fiber .25g, Sugar 12g, Protein 6g, Fat 4g, Sodium 189mg
- **DIABETIC EXCHANGES:** 1 Low-Fat Milk

MOM'S CHOICE

My husband and I are the proud parents of a handsome son, Denard. He was a beautiful baby but cried continuously from the day he was born until he was four weeks old. At that time, we learned that he was allergic to milk. We tried several formulas with unsuccessful results and as a last resort, his pediatrician recommended soy milk. I prayed that this formula would work for him, and it did.

The following years were very challenging for our family. I observed that whenever we visited his grandmother's farm, he had allergic reactions to fresh hen eggs, and I soon learned that he was also allergic to corn products. In addition to these food allergies, he developed asthma.

As Denard grew, I learned more about the ways in which foods affected his asthma and allergies. I packed his lunch daily, being careful to include only nutritional foods such as natural applesauce, raisins, and turkey sandwiches on wheat bread. Since that time, I have learned that Denard is also allergic to wheat and cannot have milks or foods that contain red dye.

For the most part, Denard accepted his fate, and as I learned more about foods that impacted his allergies, Denard's diet became so bland that he could not even have popcorn at the movies. Sometimes at school he would intentionally get chocolate milk, but the children would tell on him—the teacher had asked the other students to help her monitor students with special diets.

I had thought that by removing all of the foods that he was allergic to, Denard would outgrow his allergies, but this did not happen. At the same time, I didn't want him to miss having sweets throughout his childhood, so I began developing some healthy recipes he could enjoy.

The first thing we did was to replace milk with soy milk, which was easy to do because I am also lactose intolerant. We can now enjoy soy ice cream, and I no longer have to worry that he will sneak any of those "no-no" desserts.

That was the beginning of the development for the recipes in "Mom's Choice." Despite his allergies, I wanted my son to be able to have his favorite cakes, ice creams, smoothies, and cookies. Now, I'd like to share these yummy dessert recipes so that you and your children can enjoy them, too.

Another reason I developed these recipes was to help busy moms provide delicious, healthy desserts and snacks for their children. Children need nutrients throughout the day for schoolwork, to participate in extracurricular activities, and to complete homework. Many of these recipes can be eaten for breakfast, lunch, or as a healthy snack.

Baked Cinnamon Raisin Apple

MAKES 1 SERVING, 149 GRAMS

1 medium apple
1 tablespoon raisins
½ teaspoon ground cinnamon

Preheat oven to 350 degrees. Wrap apple in aluminum foil; bake for 20 minutes. Dust raisins with cinnamon; set aside. Unwrap baked apple, cut in half and remove the core. Replace core with raisin/cinnamon mixture. Return to oven and bake 10 additional minutes. Let cool before serving.

● **NUTRITIONAL INFORMATION PER SERVING:**
Calories 117, Carbohydrates 30g, Fiber 5g, Sugar 24g, Protein .5g, Fat .5g, Sodium 3mg
● **DIABETIC EXCHANGES:** 2 Fruit

Patty Whack Stewed Pear

MAKES 2 SERVINGS, 196 GRAMS PER SERVING

Cut pears into quarters; place in saucepan. Cover with apple cider, optional sugar, and cloves.

Bring mixture to a boil and simmer for 15 minutes. Remove pears with a slotted spoon. These are delicious served warm or cold.

2 small pears, peeled and cored

½ cup unsweetened apple cider

1 teaspoon sugar, optional

½ teaspoon ground cloves

● **NUTRITIONAL INFORMATION PER SERVING:**
Calories 114, Carbohydrates 29g, Fiber 4g, Sugar 21g, Protein 1g, Fat 1g, Sodium 8mg

● **DIABETIC EXCHANGES:** 2 Fruit

A Sweeter Sweet Potato

2 medium sweet potatoes
1 teaspoon canola oil
½ teaspoon ground cinnamon
1 tablespoon unsweetened
    applesauce

Heat oven to 375 degrees. Rub potatoes with oil; wrap in aluminum foil. Place potatoes on baking sheet and bake for 50 to 60 minutes.

Remove potatoes from oven, unwrap and cut in half. Dust potatoes with cinnamon and top each half with a dollop of applesauce. Serve warm or cold.

● **NUTRITIONAL INFORMATION PER SERVING:**
Calories 184, Carbohydrates 38g, Fiber 3g, Sugar 18g, Protein 3g,
Fat 3g, Sodium 20mg

Banana Split Pop

MAKES 1 SERVING, 143 GRAMS

Wrap banana in foil and freeze until solid. Pour melted chocolate over frozen banana. Roll chocolate-covered banana into crushed nuts. Let set for several minutes in the refrigerator before serving.

1 medium banana, peeled

½ ounce semisweet natural chocolate, melted

1½ tablespoons crushed peanuts or pecans

• NUTRITIONAL INFORMATION PER SERVING:

Calories 253, Carbohydrates 36g, Fiber 4g, Sugar 23g, Protein 3g, Fat 14g, Sodium 2mg

Berry Berry Smoothie

MAKES 2 SERVINGS, 168 GRAMS PER SERVING

¾ cup unflavored soy milk, chilled
¼ cup plain low-fat yogurt
¼ cup strawberry slices
¼ cup blueberries
2 teaspoons natural sugar
1 teaspoon vanilla extract

Place all ingredients in blender and blend until smooth.

• **NUTRITIONAL INFORMATION PER SERVING:**
Calories 88, Carbohydrates 12g, Fiber 2g, Sugar 9g, Protein 4g, Fat 2g, Sodium 34mg
• **DIABETIC EXCHANGES:** 1 Skim Milk

Variation:

Dairy-Free

MAKES 2 SERVINGS, 168 GRAMS PER SERVING

Substitute ¼ cup nondairy yogurt substitute for low-fat yogurt.

• **NUTRITIONAL INFORMATION PER SERVING:**
Calories 106, Carbohydrates 17g, Fiber 2g, Sugar 7g, Protein 4g, Fat 2g, Sodium 36mg
• **DIABETIC EXCHANGES:** 1 Fruit ½ Skim Milk

Tropical Smoothie

Place all ingredients in blender and blend until smooth.

- **NUTRITIONAL INFORMATION PER SERVING:**
Calories 176, Carbohydrates 26g, Fiber 3g, Sugar 21g, Protein 4g, Fat 6g, Sodium 44mg
- **DIABETIC EXCHANGES:** 1 Starch, 1 Skim Milk

¾ cup unflavored soy milk, chilled
¼ cup plain low-fat yogurt
1 (8-ounce) can unsweetened crushed pineapple and its juice
¼ cup frozen or fresh unsweetened coconut
2 teaspoons natural sugar
1 teaspoon coconut extract
½ teaspoon almond extract

Variation:

Dairy-Free

MAKES 2 SERVINGS, 253 GRAMS PER SERVING

Substitute ¼ cup nondairy yogurt for low-fat yogurt.

- **NUTRITIONAL INFORMATION PER SERVING:**
Calories 193, Carbohydrates 30g, Fiber 3g, Sugar 19g, Protein 4g, Fat 6g, Sodium 46mg
- **DIABETIC EXCHANGES:** 1 Starch, 1 Low-Fat Milk

Banana Granola Smoothie

MAKES 2 SERVINGS, 201 GRAMS PER SERVING

¾ cup vanilla soy milk, chilled
¼ cup plain low-fat yogurt
1 small banana
½ cup natural granola crumbs
2 teaspoons natural sugar
1 teaspoon vanilla extract

Place all ingredients in blender and blend until smooth.

● **NUTRITIONAL INFORMATION PER SERVING:**
Calories 206, Carbohydrates 39g, Fiber 2g, Sugar 25g, Protein 6g, Fat 3g, Sodium 113mg

Variation:

Dairy-Free

MAKES 2 SERVINGS, 201 GRAMS PER SERVING

Substitute ¼ cup nondairy yogurt for low-fat yogurt.

● **NUTRITIONAL INFORMATION PER SERVING:**
Calories 224, Carbohydrates 43g, Fiber 2g, Sugar 23g, Protein 6g, Fat 3g, Sodium 115mg

Strawberry and Banana Smoothie

MAKES 2 SERVINGS, 252 GRAMS PER SERVING

Place all ingredients in a blender and blend until mixture is smooth.

¾ cup soy milk, chilled

½ cup plain low-fat yogurt

1 small banana

½ cup fresh or frozen strawberry slices

1 teaspoon vanilla extract

- **NUTRITIONAL INFORMATION PER SERVING:**
Calories 134, Carbohydrates 21g, Fiber 3g, Sugar 16g, Protein 6.5g, Fat 3g, Sodium 55mg
- **DIABETIC EXCHANGES:** ½ Fruit, 1 Skim Milk

Variation:

Dairy-Free

MAKES 2 SERVINGS, 201 GRAMS PER SERVING

Substitute ½ cup nondairy yogurt for low-fat yogurt.

- **NUTRITIONAL INFORMATION PER SERVING:**
Calories 169, Carbohydrates 30g, Fiber 3g, Sugar 12g, Protein 6g, Fat 3g, Sodium 59mg
- **DIABETIC EXCHANGES:** 1 Fruit, 1 Low-Fat Milk

Apple Butter Baskets

2 packaged puff pastry or flaky
   pastry shells made with
   unbleached white flour
2 tablespoons natural apple
   butter preserves
¼ cup walnuts

Preheat oven to 400 degrees. Place pastry shell on baking sheet and bake for 20 minutes. Remove from oven.

Make an indention in the center of each shell. Spoon 1 tablespoon of apple butter in the center of each shell and sprinkle with nuts.

● **NUTRITIONAL INFORMATION PER SERVING:**
Calories 346, Carbohydrates 30g, Fiber 3g, Sugar 5g, Protein 5g,
Fat 24g, Sodium 136mg

"Color Me Kids" Gelatin Squiggles

MAKES 12 SHAPES, 90 GRAMS PER SERVING

A fun recipe that parents or classroom teachers will have fun making with their children or students. I originally created this recipe as a science lesson. Gelatin starts out as a liquid and becomes a solid. You can use apple, orange, grape, or pineapple juice, which gives you a variety of taste and color. The best part about this lesson is you get to eat it when it is complete!

Sprinkle Emes Kosher-Jel into a medium bowl; add cold juice. Do not stir; let mixture rest for 1 minute. Stir in hot juice and mix well. Blend in sugar. Add fruit. Pour into animal-shaped molds. Refrigerate until firm.

4 envelopes unflavored Emes Kosher-Jel or unsweetened gelatin

1 cup organic fruit juice, chilled

3 cups organic fruit juice, heated

2 tablespoons natural sugar

½ cup chopped fresh or frozen fruit, no sugar added

● **NUTRITIONAL INFORMATION PER SERVING:**
Calories 54, Carbohydrates 11g, Fiber 0g, Sugar 11g, Protein 2g, Fat 0g, Sodium 5mg

● **DIABETIC EXCHANGES:** 1 Other Carbohydrate

Carrot Cake Muffins

2½ cups all-purpose
   unbleached organic flour

2 teaspoons baking powder

1 teaspoon baking soda

2 teaspoons cinnamon

1½ cups natural sugar

1 teaspoon salt (optional)

4 organic eggs

2 teaspoons vanilla extract

½ cup water

¾ cup canola oil

3 cups grated carrots

½ cup crushed walnuts

Preheat oven to 375 degrees. Line muffin cups with paper liners; set aside. Sift together flour, baking powder, baking soda, cinnamon, sugar, and salt (if desired); set aside.

Using a whisk, beat eggs until frothy. Blend in vanilla extract and water. Slowly pour in oil and whisk until mixture is well combined.

Pour carrots and crushed nuts on top of sifted flour mixture; do not stir. Spoon egg mixture over flour mixture. Use the whisk to blend ingredients into a smooth batter. Immediately spoon batter into prepared muffin cups.

Bake for 20 minutes or until golden and muffins begin to pull away from the liners. Place pan on wire rack to cool for 5 to 10 minutes.

● **NUTRITIONAL INFORMATION PER SERVING:**
Calories 263, Carbohydrates 33g, Fiber 1g, Sugar 18g, Protein 4g, Fat 13g, Sodium 135mg

Heavenly Chocolate Muffins

MAKES 18 MUFFINS, 83 GRAMS PER SERVING

Preheat oven to 350 degrees. Line muffin cups with paper liners; set aside.

Sift unbleached flour and oat flour together first, then sift them with cocoa, sugar, baking powder, and baking soda; set aside. Whisk together milk, vinegar, vanilla extract, lemon extract, and water. Add eggs, 1 at a time, beating well after each addition. Add melted margarine, whisking to blend well. Pour egg mixture over sifted dry ingredients. Use the whisk to blend ingredients into a smooth batter.

Immediately spoon batter into prepared muffin tins. Bake for 20 minutes. Place pan on wire rack to cool for 5 to 10 minutes.

• **NUTRITIONAL INFORMATION PER SERVING:**
Calories 238, Carbohydrates 35g, Fiber 3g, Sugar 18g, Protein 7g, Fat 7g, Sodium 179mg

1½ cups unbleached all-purpose white flour
1 cup oat flour
½ cup Dutch-processed cocoa
1½ cups natural sugar
1½ teaspoons baking powder
1 teaspoon baking soda
½ cup soy milk
1 tablespoon apple cider vinegar
2 teaspoons vanilla extract
1 teaspoon lemon extract
1 cup cold water
4 organic eggs
1 cup soy margarine, melted

Heavenly Chocolate Egg-Free Muffins

MAKES 16 MUFFINS, 89 GRAMS PER SERVING

1½ cups unbleached all-
  purpose white flour
1 cup oat flour
½ cup Dutch-processed cocoa
  powder
1½ cups natural sugar
1 teaspoon baking powder
2 teaspoons baking soda
1 cup soy milk
2 tablespoons apple cider
  vinegar
2 teaspoons vanilla extract
1 teaspoon lemon extract
1 cup cold water
1 cup soy margarine, melted

Preheat oven to 375 degrees. Line muffin cups with paper liners; set aside. Sift unbleached flour and oat flour together first, then sift them with cocoa powder, sugar, baking powder, and baking soda; set aside.

Whisk together milk, vinegar, vanilla extract, lemon extract, and water. Add melted butter, whisking to blend well. Pour vinegar mixture over sifted dry ingredients. Use the whisk to blend ingredients into a smooth batter. Immediately spoon batter into prepared muffin tins.

Bake for 20 minutes. Place pan on wire rack to cool for 5 to 10 minutes.

● **NUTRITIONAL INFORMATION PER SERVING:**
Calories 251, Carbohydrates 39g, Fiber 3g, Sugar 20g, Protein 7g, Fat 7g, Sodium 252mg

RESOURCES

American Natural Snacks
St. Augustine, FL 32085

Arrowhead Mills, Inc.
P.O. Box 2059
Hereford, TX 79045
1-800-434-4246
Pastry flour
Stone ground flour
All-purpose baking mix

Better Than Milk
Division of Fuller Life, Inc.
1628 Robert C. Jackson Drive
Maryville, TN 37801
1-800-227-2320
Vegan beverage mix
Better Than Milk

Bob's Red Mill Natural Foods
5209 S. E. International Way
Milwaukie, OR 97222
1-503-654-3215
Whole wheat flour
Unbleached flour

Country Choice Nature
P.O. Box 44247
Minneapolis, MN 55349
Country Choice Vanilla Wafers

Delicious Brands, Inc.
2070 Maple Street
Des Plaines, IL 60018
Frookie (All Natural Wafer)

Ener-g-Foods, Inc.
P.O. Box 84487
Seattle, WA 98124-5787
1-800-331-5222
www.ener-g.com
Egg Replacer

Fearn Natural Foods
Division of Modern Products, Inc.
Milwaukee, WI 53029
Fearn Naturally Flavored Cake Mix

Florida Crystal
www.FloridaCrystal.com
Natural sugar-milled cane

Haines Pure Food
734 Franklin Ave # 444
Garden City, NY 11530
1-800-434-4246
Turbinado sugar
All-purpose natural sweetener

King Flour Company
Box 1010
Norwich, VT 05055
www.KingArthurFlour.com
King Arthur Flour
Unbleached all-purpose flour
Unbleached special bread flour

Morinaga Nutritional Food, Inc.
2050 W. 190th St., 110
Torrance, CA 90504
www.Morinu.com
Silken tofu

Tofutti Brands, Inc.
Cranford, NJ
1-800-956-6624
Tofutti Better Than Cream Cheese

White Wave, Inc.
www.SilkIsSoy.com
Boulder, CO 80301

Shedd's
Lisle, IL
1-800-735-3554
Willow Run Soybean Margarine

Whole Foods Market
For a list of locations nationwide, contact
corporate headquarters at 512-477-4455
or visit their website at
www.wholefoods.com

Wild Oats Market
For a list of locations nationwide, contact
their hotline at 1-800-494-WILD or
www.wildoats.com

SELECTED BIBLIOGRAPHY

Andrus, Mindy, and Frazier-Leggett, Nancy. "Diabetes Primer." *Diabetes Forecast.* Mar. 2002: 63–67.

Appleton, Nancy, Ph.D. *Lick the Sugar Habit.* New York: Avery Publishing Group, 1996.

Better Homes and Gardens New Baking Book. Des Moines, IA: Meredith Publishing Group, 1998.

Buhr, Deborah. *The "I Can't Believe This Has No Sugar" Cookbook.* New York: St. Martin's Griffin, 1997.

Costigan, Fran. *Great Good Desserts.* New York: Good Cakes Production, 1999.

Diabetic Cooking. "For the Way You Live." May/June 2002: 6–7.

Dufty, William F. *Sugar Blues.* New York: Warner Books Inc., 1976.

Evers, Connie. *How to Teach Nutrition to Kids: An Integrated, Creative Approach to Nutrition Education for Children Ages 6–10.* Oregon: 24 Carrot Press, 1995.

Gaines, Fabiola D., and Weaver, Ronice. *The New Soul Food Cookbook for People with Diabetes.* New York: McGraw-Hill, 1999.

Gittleman, Ann Louise. *Get the Sugar Out: 501 Simple Ways to Cut the Sugar in Any Diet.* New York: Three River Press, 1996.

Goodman, Donna. *Somethin' to Shout About!* Stone Mountain, GA: Remnant Publications, 1999.

Hamilton, E. M., Whitney, E., and Sizer, F. *Nutrition Concept and Controversies,* 4th ed. New York: West Publishing Company, 1988.

Holt, Stephen. *The Soy Revolution: The Food for the Next Millennium.* New York: Dell Publishing, 1998.

Jenson, Bernard. *Dr. Jensen's Guide to Natural Weight Control: A Balanced Approach to Well-Being.* New York: Keats Publishing, 2000.

La Place, Viana. *Desserts and Sweet Snacks: Rustic, Italian Style.* New York: Morrow Cookbooks, 1998.

Lobue, Andrea, and Marsea, Marcus. *The Don't Diet Live-it Workbook.* Carlsbad, CA: Gurze Books, 1999.

Meyer, J. *Eat and Stay Thin: Simple, Spiritual, Satisfaction Weight Control.* Tulsa, OK: Harrison House, Inc., 2000.

Oser, Marie. *Soy of Cooking: Easy-to-Make Vegetarian, Low-Fat, Fat-Free, and Antioxidant-Rich Gourmet Recipes.* New York: John Wiley & Sons, 1996.

Rohde, Betty. *So Fat, Low Fat, No Fat Desserts: More Than 160 Recipes from the Best-selling Author of So Fat, Low Fat, No Fat.* New York: Fireside, 1999.

Sheppard, Kay. *Food Addiction: The Body Knows.* Deerfield Beach, FL: Health Communications, Inc., 1989.

The Southern Living Cookbook. Birmingham, AL: Oxmoor House, Inc., 1987.

Weil, Andrew, and Daley, Rosie. *The Healthy Kitchen: Recipes for a Better Body, Life, and Spirit.* New York: Random House, 2002.

Williams, Jack, and Silverman, Goldie. *No Salt, No Sugar, No Fat.* San Leandro, CA: Briston Publishing Enterprises, 1993.

INDEX

ABOUT THE AUTHOR

Dr. Yvonne Butler-Sanders is the principal of the one thousand–student Brown Mills Arts and Magnet School in Lithonia, Georgia. She has been actively involved in education and counseling for more than seventeen years. As school principal, Dr. Butler made improving her students' health a top priority. She established her school's Nutrition and Excellence program, which took sugar, high fat, and processed foods and drinks off the school menu.

Dr. Butler is the founder of Ennovy, Inc., a company providing workshops, seminars, wellness consultation, and maintenance using spiritual awareness, sound nutrition practices, and physical activities to achieve wellness. When she's not at school, she enjoys lecturing, cooking, and spending time with her family on their horse farm in Georgia.